The Voice and the Word

The Voice and the Word

*What One Priest Learned
from the Homilies He Preached*

Vincent John Fecher

VANTAGE PRESS
New York

Cover design by Susan Thomas

FIRST EDITION

Published by Vantage Press, Inc.
419 Park Ave. South, New York, NY 10016

Manufactured in the United States of America
ISBN: 0-533-15206-2

Library of Congress Catalog Card No.: 2005902685

0 9 8 7 6 5 4 3 2 1

Contents

Foreword   vii

Part One: Awareness of the Word
The Voice and the Word   3
Short Prayers   11
Getting to Know Him   24
What He Actually Said Was . . .   39
Liturgy—Serving God and Community   53

Part Two: Selected Homilies for Feasts
Preaching the Voice and the Word   67
Advent—First Sunday   69
Christmas from Luke 2   73
Epiphany   76
Baptism of Christ   80
The Tempting of Christ   84
The Vine and the Branches   88
Easter   92
Thomas Doubting, Then Believing   97
Peter Goes Fishing   100
The Ascension   104
Pentecost   109
Corpus Christi   113
The Christ of God   117
The Prodigal Son   121
Casting the First Stone   125

Foreword

The Book and the Title:

The writer of these pages believes that the title and the content of a book or film ought to be related to each other. Furthermore, that the alleged relationship ought to be clear to anyone expected to read the book or to watch the film, after learning its title. (There may be something inherently clever about paper moons and water for chocolate; but when these words were used as titles, some of us at least could find no connection between the title and that-which-was-so-entitled.)

As used in our own title, "THE WORD," is the Word of God. Specifically The Word as He became incarnate—the Word "in-the-flesh," to borrow our phrasing from St. John's Gospel Prologue. Incarnate, enfleshed, the Word Who dwelt amongst us as Jesus Christ. Truly Son of God and Son of Man, while still THE WORD; and no less Word for being the Word Incarnate.

As Son of Man, He spoke with a human voice. Some people listened and some did not. Those who did listen, those who believed in Him, were given a share in His Sonship; and they themselves became children of God. One such believer penned an inspired description of his resulting state-of-being, summing up life after having been encountered by Christ : "It's not just 'me' living any more; CHRIST is living in me. My natural bodily life does go on, of course; only now it is steered by faith. Faith in the Son of God, Who loved me (that is: Who wanted me)" (Gal. 2:20).

Nothing strange then, if The Word Who is living on in other

vii

human beings should sometimes speak with their voices. Our thesis in this book, our premise and presupposition is that Christ *can and does* use the voices of those in whom He lives. Often, but not always, He will use their voices, as once He used His unique individual human voice. Uses them in speaking to proclaim the kingdom of God: just as He Himself did two thousand years ago.

That will be the case, particularly but neither exclusively nor always, whenever the human voice concerned is that of someone preaching. Someone who in a smaller way continues Christ's own proclaiming of the Gospel and of the Kingdom. The "Voice" in our title. A voice sensitive to the presence of the Lord, a voice surrendered to Him utterly, a voice for Him to use.

So the Voice is not just *any* voice, nor will it be just anything that this particular person says, even if he or she says it in a sermon form. The beaches of Church history are littered with wretched wrecks made of the Gospel by miscellaneous heretical preachers, even though those preachers may have thought that they were actually speaking in the name of God.

And yet, there is something very real going on here; and if it sometimes goes wrong, that should not blind us to the many times it goes right. People who listen to the Voice are often touched by The Word. Moreover, the Voice itself gains new insights into Scripture, gains a new and clearer understanding of the word-of-God-in-a-book. New insights into the "personality" of the Word-made-flesh-and-dwelling-among-us. His "Person" is divine, the Second Person of the Trinity. His "personality" is human, the set of traits that describe what Jesus Christ was like when He walked this earth. What He WAS like, and IS like yet: yesterday, today, and forever unchanged (Heb. 13:8).

So the title of this book is, "The Voice and the Word." Its subtitle might be expanded to read not only "What one priest learned from the homilies he preached," but also: "What he learned about the Gospels and about the Christ of the Gospels, learned about being a priest and a preacher, as well as about being a Christian."

Though cumbersome as a subtitle, it might resemble those title pages they published a hundred years ago, title pages that told you plainly what the book was really all about.

The Book and the Reader:

For whom is this book intended? Who might want to read it, and who might profit thereby? Not only priests. Not only those who preach. Our hope in writing it is that The Word may also make use of this book to "reach out and touch someone." That the book itself, and the writer's story it tells, may be instrumental in moving some readers to take a fresh look at the Gospels, to yearn for and to strive for a more personal acquaintance with Christ the Lord.

True, the latter part of the book is in the form of homilies. Fifteen homilies that were actually preached in this form to the People of God in some Texas parish. Fifteen homilies, all of which contain some reading of the scriptures that the homilist did not discover already in print. Fifteen homilies offered as a "for instance" aimed at illustrating statements made in initial chapters of this book. Fifteen homilies that (the present writer would like to think) have been co-authored by the Word and by the Voice, both of us working together.

However, it would be a mistake to advertise this book as a mini-collection of homilies. For one thing, it wouldn't sell. Many active preachers would not even dip into it. Why? Because most priests or deacons or other preachers who are searching for homiletic material would prefer to go for a complete liturgical year or cycle. Preference would also be given, probably, to some scholarly Bible author who might be sophisticated enough to express doubts about the scripture text, its provenance, and the "possible" late date of its composition. It would be foolhardy for a retired country pastor to compete with such scholars (even with a couple graduate degrees from four universities in his own pocket, because none of those degrees were in the field of biblical studies!).

So the Retired Country Pastor would like to see the present slim little volume presented this way: It is a book of Christ-centered spiritual reading, a book of meditations to help the grass-roots faithful to see many a Gospel scene in a new light. And perhaps the chapters, on "Short Prayers" and on "Getting to Know Him" may even move some people to become more intimate with the Lord Christ Himself.

Verily, "a consummation devoutly to be wished"—to borrow and alter the words of Hamlet. This writer ("the Voice") only wishes it had not taken him eighty years to discover what life is all about. Now at least he would like to share with fellow travelers and with fellow seekers the vision visible from his particular hilltop.

That is the why and the wherefore of this little book. Into Thy hands, O Lord! Use it on someone, won't You? Please??

The Voice and the Word

Part One

Awareness of the Word

The Voice and the Word
Or: What One Priest Learned
from the Homilies He Preached

Preliminary Remarks

This book—if it ever grows up to be one—is not about me, but about HIM. Not about the Voice, but about the Word. The Word that was in the beginning with God. The Word that WAS God. WAS, and still IS.

As for the Voice in question, like all voices everywhere, it will eventually fade away into silence. Whereas the Word of God remains, as it will remain forever (1 Pt. 1:25).

Besides the Word-of-God-in-Person, we are also concerned here with the Word-of-God-in-the-Book, the Bible. Especially the Gospels, which tell about Christ. Let it be noted up front that the reflections on Sacred Scripture presented in these pages are not primarily presented as the thoughts and utterances of a particular priest, who happened to learn them, one day or other, by preaching homilies. Whatever is good and true in these reflections, whatever is light-giving and life-giving, stems from the Word, not from the Voice. Not from this particular priest.

For this particular priest, like any preacher anywhere, knows full well that he himself is *not* the Light. A good preacher's job is rather to be like a lens that gathers the Light. Gathers it and focuses it: focuses it on this or that congregation of individual hearers, without knowing who, if anyone, among them is going to be affected by what is being said.

3

The lens itself is aware of the Light. Sometimes, very much so. Though rarely, if ever, aware whose life the Light is enlightening at any given moment. After all, that is HIS business. That is HIS department. For HE is the actual Light, the real Light, which shines as It will, upon those who sit in darkness and in the shadows.

Our position on all this is that there is a very close and a very real collaboration going on between the Voice and the Word, between the priest and the High Priest, the lens and the Light. Over the years, this conviction has grown very strong and very vivid for the priest/preacher who pens these lines. It is a conviction that dawned upon him only gradually, beginning some thirty-five years ago and half a world away.

At that time, when the dawn broke, he had already been a priest for over twenty years, during all of which time he had worked hard at honing his preaching skills. None of it, neither the effort nor the experience, prepared him for what happened to his life and his preaching then, at a workers' parish on the rim of Rome, in the aftermath of Vatican II.

It all began not so much in his seminary years (the 1940s), but afterward—months after his ordination, when he first got a chance to preach to the People of God, and was appalled at the terrible job he was doing. Several years of graduate studies followed, during which time academic matters clamored for his attention. Yet even then, as a student priest in Rome, wherever two or three were gathered together to listen to a sermon, a lecture, or a Communist harangue (it was the fifties!), there he was in the midst of them.

Launching into a ten-year seminary teaching career, he made time to read every book on sacred and profane oratory that he could lay his hands on. Ransacked the library where he taught, gleaning ideas for inclusion into next Sunday's sermon at a nearby suburban parish church. (Yes, "sermon." There were as yet no homilies; only sermons. Sermons whose subject matter was rigidly regulated by each diocese, so as to cover all Church teachings on the Creed, the Commandments, the Sacraments, and—big indeed in those three decades preceding Vatican II—the Social Doctrine of the Church.)

Once the sermon had been typed up, it invariably proved too long for the fifteen-minute goal laid down by pastors as the limit. The parts that were cut out, however reluctantly, always seemed to be library material, so painstakingly researched.

The slimmed-down manuscript was borne up into the seminary attic, to be declaimed at top volume in front of a full-length mirror, to critique the gestures as well as the sound. For five years, every sermon was vetted by resident bats and mice, forced to hear it twenty to twenty-five times before anyone heard it in church.

For the next five years, both seminary teaching and parish preaching were continued in Southeast Asia; and the sermons were practiced, in English or Tagalog, amid bamboo groves inhabited by miscellaneous lizards.

The next move was to an office job in Rome. Through the providence of God, it proved possible to spend Sunday mornings helping out pastorally, helping an overworked Italian parish priest who had about 10,000 people in his territory. The sermons from the very outset, and later the liturgical prayers, were of course in Italian. Which meant that practicing a sermon out loud two dozen times had to continue, though in different surroundings.

Then one day, also providentially, he encountered a German layman who proved rather critical and rather vocal about the quality of Sunday preaching in his own country. "What is it that you want in a sermon?" he was asked. The answer came back without a moment's hesitation: *Das Wort Gottes*—the Word of God!" He said he wanted to know what "the word of God" meant in itself, and then what it might mean for him, in his own life. That seemed like a good formula to follow, both then and ever after.

Meanwhile, Vatican II, just ended, had induced a liturgical reform with more emphasis on the Scriptures. It prescribed that the homily was generally to comment on the weekly scripture selections: all part of the newly discovered Liturgy of the Word.

Thus it happened that both the Council and the German layman brought about a major change in the preaching of this one priest, then twenty years ordained. From now on, the subject matter of his "homilies" would definitely be Scripture. Particularly the Gospel Readings, conveniently arranged in Cycles A, B, and C.

Moreover, the liturgical reform of Vatican II had another and even more radical effect, so far as this particular priest was concerned. The altar had been dutifully turned around, so that he faced the people while saying in their mother tongue, "*Questo è il mio corpo* . . . This is My Body!*"

Surprisingly enough, his own reaction was: "Hey! This ain't MY body!" Surprising, because he had known all his life what "*Hoc est enim Corpus Meum*" meant, that these were the words of Christ and that the resulting Body was also that of Christ. It was only that the apparent disconnect between what he was saying and what was happening never struck him so forcibly as it did now, when he had to say those words to Italians in Italian—a language otherwise used only to communicate information, to get an idea across.

And yet, however clear this feeling of a "disconnect" might have been, the answer dawned upon him more clearly still, as if it were Christ Himself Who patiently explained, "No, not YOUR body. Mine. It is indeed your voice that is saying this, but that's because I am the One using your voice. Using your voice to speak and to act. Since I am the one speaking (with your voice), it's really MY body that we're talking about here. Mine: not yours. I am borrowing your voice to say 'My Body' much as you might borrow a pen to write your name, to sign a credit card receipt. The pen may be borrowed from a shopkeeper, but the signature is yours, the responsibility is yours, whoever might own the pen. When I use your voice to declare the bread to be MY Body, then it IS My

Body. Mine. Just like it's your signature, though written by an alien pen."

Master, I feel like the Samaritan woman who prayed, "Give me always this water" (Jn. 4:15)! She probably did not realize what she was asking for; but she did want it, and she got it. "Always." Or like Peter at the Last Supper: Peter who was never one to stop halfway. "In that case, Lord, not only my feet but also my hands and my head" (Jn. 13:9). So if You're going to use my voice at the consecration, Lord, why not use it in the confessional too? And maybe in the pulpit as well . . . ?

From what followed, it seems that the Lord took him up on it. In the confessional, through hours and hours of penitents, it was Christ Who understood and empathized, it was Christ who loved and forgave. That is another chapter. The pertinent part here is, that the Lord used the voice of one very ordinary priest to say some very extraordinary things, to preach homilies that were far out of his league, homilies containing insights that had never ever occurred to him before. . . . Nor did they seem to have occurred to any of the scholars, the ones who published their own brilliant analyses of the scripture texts under consideration.

Though the priest was not aware of it just then, no less an authority than the Second Vatican Council had already declared, in its 1963 Constitution on the Sacred Liturgy (Sacrosanctum Concilium n. 7), that "Christ is present in the sacrifice of the Mass in the person of His minister. . . . He is present in the sacraments, so that when a man baptizes, it is really Christ Himself Who baptizes. He is present in His word, since it is He Himself Who speaks when the Holy Scriptures are read in church." Present in the sacraments. So they might have added (besides the mention of baptism) that it is really Christ Who consecrates, Christ Who absolves. And in addition to mentioning Him speaking when the Scriptures are read, it might have been added that He also speaks when Scriptures are officially commented on. Christ Who speaks in the homily.

In those early days, when this priest got down to preparing the homily, he sometimes drew a complete blank: writer's block. That may not have been so accidental. Perhaps it was willed by the Lord Christ, so that there would be no doubt about who was doing this! In any event, upon approaching the pulpit some Sundays, the prayer of the priest went something like this: "Lord, I hope You have something to say to them. Because You know darned well I haven't!! I tried, but I came up empty. Please take over!?"

The homilies that then issued forth from the mouth of the writer's-blocked priest not only had hands and feet (a German expression). They were precisely the ones after which people would say, upon exiting the church: "Thanks! I needed that. . . ."

Both at such times, and on other occasions as well, the priest himself marveled at some brand new insight, some deeper understanding of how the things of God are interconnected. He preached to the people, but inwardly he said to himself: "I never realized that!" People told him, and still tell him, that they have learned from his homilies. He himself has learned even more.

Before we go on, let's be clear on one point (to forestall your accusations of chutzpah, of conceit, of downright arrogance). There is no pretense here of special sanctity, no claim to divine inspiration, no feeling of infallibility. No miracles are happening, no visions, no inner locutions, no voices, no apparitions. This is different. This is in a class by itself. Nevertheless, it brings with it an unmistakable sense of Christ using the voice of a priest to speak to His people.

For the priest himself, there is a grand exhilarating sense of working together with the Lord. Getting to know Him the way men get to know each other when they have worked together at something for a long time, side by side. It's not even necessary for them to talk about it. Each man knows the other man's "modus operandi," knows what the other man likes and dislikes, how he goes about doing the job. And either person's contribution to the said job seems to mesh flawlessly with that of the other. There is a certain harmony, a shared method. Genuine "collaboration."

There is an additional corollary. You begin to understand the need of getting out of the way occasionally, of not getting underfoot. Physicists have found that a metal conductor loses almost all its resistance when cooled down to absolute zero or close to it: so that an electric current runs on smoothly and endlessly through the loop. You begin to suspect that the grace of Christ will also run more smoothly when it encounters less resistance from the conducting wire, when one's own self does not get in the way. People will always tell the preacher how much they liked the homily. A good and truthful reply is always: "I'll tell the Lord you liked it. That's His department. He is the Word, I'm just the Voice." Speak your piece, like John the Baptist; then step quietly back into the penumbra. The limelight and the spotlight are for the Lord, for the Word Himself.

Gradually, you begin to see all this displayed against a wider horizon. It's not just for preaching homilies that the Lord Christ takes hold of our human nature. What is happening here is a real incarnation, an "incarnation-with-a-small-letter-i," one that plays point-and-counterpoint with that one big unique and unrepeatable "Incarnation-with-a-capital-letter-I." An incarnation whereby He comes to share in our humanity, even as we share in His divinity (offertory prayer when mixing water with the wine).

For this is a way in which He "humbles Himself to share in our humanity." He did it another way when the Person of the Word bound Himself hypostatically to one single human nature, that human (oh, so human!) nature of Our Lord Jesus Christ. Then, analogously though really, He takes hold of OUR individual humanity, lays hold of our individual versions of human nature, using all of them and each one of them in order to live human life in this world, live it to the hilt in many times and many climes.

Incarnate, "living in the flesh" of many priests and preachers, He is able to speak with myriad tongues all over the world, century

9

after century. By virtue of living in many different Christian men and women ("I live now, not I, but Christ lives in me"), He is able to drive a car, to bear children, to make music and to build cities, to farm the land and to perfect ever new forms of communication and technology, to invent new cures for human ills. In short, by sharing in OUR human nature, He is able to live human life more fully than ever, and to sanctify all of it for the glory of God.

Any Christian, in this view, can borrow the words of St. Paul to the Galatians (Gal. 2:20): "It's not just me doing this. Because I am not living this human life by myself: Christ lives in me. Christ works through me. As I live and breathe and speak and act and work and play, the Lord and I are doing this together. Doing it for the glory of God and for the salvation of the world. The salvation and the sanctification of MY world, of OUR world, His and mine, the world of the here and now. Sanctifying it in the sense of consecrating it to God, claiming it for God, so that what we are making real may be doing Him homage, glorifying His name."

By sanctifying grace, Christians share in what makes Christ the Son of God. He in turn—O wondrous exchange!—shares in our humanity. We share in what makes Him the Son of God, He shares in what makes us children of men. Shares in our human life in all its aspects, shares in what causes us humans to be human at all. Thus He continues to live out the incarnation in all of us on our level, in all Christians everywhere, whether ordained or not, whether preaching or not. All of us can glorify our Heavenly Father by what we are saying or doing. By everything that we and Christ are doing together.

Astounded, filled with awe and wonder, I say to myself, "What a wonderful world!" No: I am aware that I did not just make up that line. But I couldn't have said it better myself!

Short Prayers

Communication is vital to a relationship. Any relationship. Many a marriage has died, "not with a bang but with a whimper" (to adapt what T.S. Eliot said of the world). Died, simply because the couple quit talking to each other.

I

Our relationship with God, our relationship with Christ, also needs prayer to survive. True, such a relationship is essentially a matter of grace, and grace is a free gift of God. But paradoxically, we have to keep the lines of communication always open, or that gift will never be received.

Since prayer is so important, it is not surprising that so much has been said and written about it. Down through the centuries, real giants of the spirit have left us THEIR prayers; some have even added detailed instructions on how to make up our own. Various schools of spirituality have sprung up, parallel to the tendency that has turned Faith into a science called theology. A science, or an academic discipline.

There is also a science or art of spirituality that has evolved as well, and it can now be studied at reputable teaching centers. Today, various experts in the field are expounding any number of prayer-methods, some of which might actually work for certain people. For the rest of us, it only remains to join in the earnest plea of the Apostles: "Lord, teach us how to pray!" (Lk. 11:1).

In reply, Jesus gave them and us the "Our Father." He certainly did not mean that His followers should say only these precise words and nothing else. Rather, the "Our Father" was to be an example, a "for instance." Surely the Lord Jesus will not be displeased with us if we explore His own Gospel for tips on how to pray well.

One important clue comes from Christ Himself in His Sermon on the Mount—when you pray, keep it short (Mt. 6:7). Don't try to impress God with your eloquence, like the pagans do. Skip the details. Your Heavenly Father knows your needs, far better than you do. He understands the problem: no need to explain it for Him. Nor does He need directions from us as to how He ought to proceed with a solution: "Please take care of this and of that, but beware! You'll have to watch out lest such-and-such happen . . ." After all, He is God. He might very well interrupt our careful planning and ask, "Who's doing this, anyway?" You don't tell God how to do his job.

Keep it short. The anonymous author of *The Cloud of Unknowing* makes the point that people talk least when their feelings are at their strongest. When there is a real sense of urgency, like when a non-swimmer falls into a river or when the house is on fire, you won't hear people making speeches. "Help!" or, "Fire!" is all they say, and all they need to say.

Another anonymous author ("The Way of the Pilgrim") got much mileage out of the Jesus Prayer. Which is a very short generic prayer, lifted straight out of the Gospels, simply repeated over and over again, with no superfluous embroidery. "Jesus, Son of David, have pity on me!" Straight to the point. Inspired. And efficacious. It worked for Gospel people (Mt. 9:27 and 15:22; Mk. 10:47; Lk. 18:38). Why shouldn't it work for us?

Short prayers have the advantage of fitting neatly into our short attention spans, so distractions will not be a problem. They also set off a mechanism which psychologists (and also *Webster's Dictionary*) call perseveration: "spontaneous recurrence" of a thought, like a tune that keeps running through your mind. Almost automatically, you catch yourself repeating your latest thought: "My Jesus mercy! Jesus Son of David have pity on me!" A good short prayer comes with a built-in prompt that makes it pop up in your consciousness again just a few minutes later. Truly a way to "pray always" (Lk. 18:1). A way to pray non-stop (1 Th. 5:17).

Old timers, particularly those schooled by consecrated women a couple generations ago, will recognize the kind of kid-sized prayers they taught us then. "My Jesus mercy." "Sweet Heart of Mary, be my salvation." "Jesus, Mary Joseph." "All for the greater honor and glory of God." Some of those prayers, like the prayer of St. Thomas ("My Lord and my God!"), came straight out of the Bible. Like the "Jesus Prayer." Inspired by such examples, let us "search the Scriptures" for other short prayers, prayers that will need little or no "processing", that can be used just as they are.

When you read the Bible, you can mentally run the stream of Scripture through sluices and separate out the gold dust that is there, mixed with a certain amount of sand. That is good, that is wise. Better and wiser, though, would be to search for nuggets of pure gold that can be plucked out of the stream and used just as they are, without changing a word. Short, golden prayers that can be applied to something currently happening in your own life. The very way those prayers are formulated, they will fit a variety of cases. Winged words that render our own sentiments exactly. "What oft was thought, but ne'er so well expressed." Even "My Lord and my God" can be interpreted (and hence can be prayed) in half a dozen different ways.

The short collection given below might furnish some examples. Each of these nuggets was discovered while thinking or talking "homiletically" about some Gospel scene that gave rise to that particular prayer. The homily itself is not reproduced here. We should also note that we are not reproducing the NAB translation of the nuggets either: that translation is copyrighted (!). Any similarities between the NAB and our own version would be due to the fact that we are all following the same original.

II

"Lord, if You just wanted to, I know You could cure me!" Thus the leper ("Hansen's disease sufferer") in Mt. 8:2. Note, it's not: "if You wish." Such a translation makes it sound as if the leper were saying, "I personally couldn't care less. But if YOU want to, go ahead!" For this poor man, the situation was a lot more serious than that, and so was his plea. That is why he was waiting for Jesus as He came down the mountain, came down from the Sermon on the Mount. That same sermon on that same mount where He had said, "Keep it short." Well, the sick man could hardly have made his prayer shorter. And the Lord's answer was just as short. Touché! You were listening, O nameless leprous friend!

(By the way: What WAS his name? What ever became of him? Never mind, says Matthew. Stick to the point.) There was nothing superfluous in that man's prayer, and nothing superfluous in Jesus' answer, which corresponded to it exactly. "If You really wanted to . . ." I DO want to! "You could do it . . ." All right, I will!

Adapting the prayer to our own private purposes, we could shorten it still further. Faced with some private concern of our own, not necessarily Hansen's disease or any other health problem, but just anything at all that worries us, we whisper to the Lord: "If You really wanted to, I know You could do something about this!" We don't even have to remind Him that there is a biblical precedent, a Gospel parallel. He will remember, and He might even appreciate the fact that we do—without even mentioning it.

"Keep it short," He said. Short prayers have more faith, more

14

hope. Keeping it short means you know you don't deserve it, and the final decision is up to Him. "Thy will be done" is understood.

Another nugget comes from Peter, who walked on top of the water until his faith began to waver (Mt. 14:28–30). When he began to sink, he cried out in panic, "Lord, save me!" Talk about prayer stripped down to its essentials!

But even before the situation got so desperate, Peter left many of us with an important lesson. A lesson, and a prayer to use when we are not so sure about leaving the comparative security of the boat. Will this rash course of action we are contemplating actually bring us closer to the Lord? Or should we just stay put, like the majority of the Apostles? "Lord, if that is really You out there in the dark and the storm, bid me come to You. Bid me come, even if it means doing the impossible, even if it means walking on the water (which I know well enough that I can't do!)."

Christ must have smiled at Peter, as He must smile at some of us Petrine wannabes. You can almost picture Jesus shaking His head out there in the darkness, lighting up the night with an amused half grin. "That Peter! Just like him!" Then aloud the Lord says, "All right! Come on!" And Peter does come . . . until Peter's faith begins to fail. No faith, no miracle. Not that faith itself CAUSES miracles. It's simply that faith is a necessary condition without which miracles just aren't going to happen.

Then there is a Canaanite woman, who hailed from the seacoast of Tyre and Sidon, in present-day Lebanon. "Help me, Lord!" she says (Mt. 15:25). And she won't take "no" for an answer.

Her story is precious and very instructive, whether you take it from Mt. 15:21–28 or from Mk. 7:24–30. In either account, she comes across as an extremely interesting person, one we'd like to know better. What was her name? Her age? Married, widowed, single parent of a daughter vexed by a demon? And the daughter? Age? Name? How did the demon vex her, and since when? Whatever became of the two, mother and daughter?

Despite a maddening lack of details, we can read a lot between the lines. About her—and about Christ (something we will reserve for another chapter). What concerns us here is only her prayer. Short. Persistent. And how cleverly she turns the Lord's own words back on Him. The very example that He had just used as a good reason for His refusal—that was the very example that she turned into a good reason for Him to grant her petition. To grant her a scrap from the children's table, even before those children had had their chance to dine at leisure and be satisfied.

Notice her prayer. Two prayers, actually. The first was shouted from a distance, to the great embarrassment of the Apostles. "Have pity on me, Son of David! My daughter is tormented by a demon." That prayer, Christ could ignore. And ignore it He did.

When she shortened it down to, "Lord, help me!" (Mt. 15:25), He could no longer resist. It was her faith that He praised as He gave in. But another reason why He gave in was her persistence. The sort of thing He Himself had recommended on other occasions. Like, "keep on knocking" (Lk. 11:8 and Lk. 18:5).

The success of this Lebanese Lady (who wouldn't take "no" for an answer) was all the more remarkable because Jesus had just told His Apostles that His mission was only to the lost sheep of the House of Israel (Mt. 15:24). She was not of their number when He said that, and she still wasn't when He worked a miracle for her anyway, just a few minutes later. In making an exception to His own "job description," Jesus must have seen a powerful reason in that faith of hers. Probably He was also favorably impressed by that quick wit of hers, that razor-sharp thrust of repartee.

Even at this distance, it impresses us. But what interests us even more in our present reflections is the very short and very useful prayer that she coined here. A generic prayer, a prayer for all occasions. Just: "Lord, help me!" It worked for her, it will work for us. For the Lord is the same, yesterday, today, and forever (Heb.

13:8). If it moved Him then, it will move Him now. We have a real, precious nugget here.

A blind man gives us another. Jesus asked him, "What do you want Me to do for you?" (Mk. 10:51). The man replied, "Lord, that I may see!"

Another short prayer, another prayer that got a miracle for an answer. Like the Lady from Lebanon (who wouldn't take "no" for an answer), this blind man of Jericho started with a shout. Like her, the prayer he shouted was "The Jesus Prayer." Like her, he kept at it stubbornly, persistently, though there were many who tried to make him keep quiet. Don't bother the Lord. Don't embarrass Jesus by handing Him a hopeless, impossible request, one that He can't possibly honor. Good people, with good intentions, tried to squelch the blind man's prayer.

Nevertheless, the blind man (like the Lady from Lebanon) shouted all the louder. And as a result, like her, he finally got the Lord's attention. And then his prayer, like hers, was a model of brevity: "That I may see!" Thus prayed the blind man, Bartimaeus. Like the Lady from Lebanon, Bartimaeus, too, got his miracle. (Mark has the name, Bartimaeus. Mark also has only ONE blind man, who is cured just as Jesus and his Apostles are LEAVING Jericho. In Matthew, there are TWO blind men, and the miracle takes place on the WAY OUT OF Jericho [Mt. 20:29–34]. Luke [18:35–43] agrees with Mark on there being ONE blind man, but he differs from both Mark and Matthew by placing the miracle on their APPROACH to Jericho, rather than when they are on their way out of town. Furthermore [just to complicate matters], Matthew apparently tells the same story twice, once in Mt. 9:27–31 prior to the first sending-out of the Twelve; and then what seems to be the same story is placed toward the end of Jesus' ministry in Mt. 20:29ff. The present writer has no idea how these diverse synoptic accounts can be reconciled; nor is he particularly worried in case no one else succeeds in really reconciling them.)

Till now, we have concentrated on short prayers that other

people made to Christ the Lord. We must not overlook the gems that were some of His own praying, especially during His Passion. Mt. 26:39 for instance, and Mt. 26:42. Both prayers were prayed in the Garden of Gethsemani: "Father, if possible, let this bitter cup pass me by. Nevertheless, let it be as You would have it, not as I!"

I'd rather this would not happen to Me, He says. But YOU decide. "Father, if this cup cannot pass away without my drinking it, Thy will be done!" Two forms of one same prayer, a prayer that just might be the hardest one of all for us to pray after Him. Hard to pray it, harder yet to really mean it.

Christ gave us another sometimes-difficult prayer in Lk. 23:34: "Father, forgive them! They know not what they do." Forgive them, don't punish them. Don't even teach them a lesson. A very handy prayer to pray when someone wrongs you, offends you, hurts you . . . or even just cuts you off too sharply at a freeway exit ramp. Instead of brooding over the idiotic act, or raging at the idiot who acted, we pray for the idiot. It is hard to be angry with someone while you are praying for them. Besides, by praying such a prayer you are in good company. In concert with the Lord.

[True, the NAB text & note would seem to cast doubt on whether this line ever formed part of Luke's original Gospel. Never mind. Even if it was not in the original manuscript, that in itself would not necessarily mean that Jesus never said it. An oral tradition may have preserved it, and eventually added it to the text. Actually, it does SOUND like Jesus. Sounds a lot like Him!]

Even better is that other prayer of Christ on the cross, found in Lk. 23:46: "Father, into Thy hands I commend my spirit!" It would be very nice indeed if these could be OUR last words, pronounced as we cross the threshold into eternity. A similar prayer was that of the dying Protomartyr St. Stephen: "Lord Jesus, receive my spirit" (Acts 7:59).

It would be a good idea to practice saying these prayers now, while we still can: for instance, at Compline (aka "Night Prayer") or just as we are falling asleep each night. After all, there is only a slim chance of our being lucid enough to pray them, fully conscious, at the moment of death. Sudden death (accident, stroke, or cardiac arrest) takes many a person by surprise.

And even if we do die of something slower like cancer, our minds might not be clear up till the last moment. Hospitals often mercifully medicate a terminal patient. As surgeons put people under a general anesthetic before removing something like an appendix or a gall bladder from a patient's body, one gets the impression that God Himself induces some blessed form of lessened awareness when He, like a Divine Surgeon, is about to remove a soul from a body. He, too, provides a sort of general anesthesia, lest His "patient" panic or worry. In any case, we would do well to pray our last adieu betimes, even pray it habitually, while we still know what we are saying.

Both the preceding examples are excellent exit lines. Another is a verse from the high-priestly prayer of Jesus at the Last Supper. "I have glorified You on earth," He says to His Heavenly Father. "I have finished the work that You gave me to do" (Jn. 17:4). Like Christ the Lord, though of course to a much lesser degree, each of us has been given something special to do on earth. In His plan, our Father and Creator has assigned to each of us a certain location and a certain function in the general scheme of things. Like so many little tiles or tesserae of a certain shape and size and color, all of us together make up the whole mosaic, the whole grand picture.

Our boast (if we have one) should be that we did our little bit, each one in our own allotted time and place. If we can be proud of anything, let it be that we did a good job of being just what God meant us to be, right where He wanted us, and when. People are often heard to say that they wanted to make a difference with their lives. That is fine, provided that is what God intended. For the ultimate criterion of a successful life will be not whether we have made a difference, but whether (like Christ) we have finished the work that God gave us to do.

John 17:4 could be an exit line. It could also be taken by moderns as a retirement prayer, along with Lk. 24:29 and Psalm 70 (71), 9 and 18. As people retire into life's long evening, they may well feel that they did finish the work that God gave them to do—finished their work, and then retired. Retired gracefully, with the prospect of many more years of living, before "the night comes, when it is impossible to work" (Jn. 9:4).

Which is all right. Retirees may, if they wish, pounce upon Jn. 17:4 as the short prayer that best befits their Golden Age. Some of us may alternate with another line from John: "Lord, You have kept the best wine till last!" (Jn. 2:10). Or that line from Lk. 24:29—"Remain with us, Lord, it is getting dark; the day is almost over." However, no one should quarrel with retirees who feel that they have earned the right to join the Lord in saying, with a touch of satisfaction that is perfectly justifiable: "O God, I have finished the work which You gave me to do in this world."

Scripture is flexible that way. The same group of words can very well have several different meanings, all of them legitimate and all of them authentically scriptural. Look at the way the Gospel of Matthew (Mt. 2:15, citing Hos. 11.1) applied a text like, "Out of Egypt I called My Son." If some scripture scholar objected to Matthew that the Old Testament prophet seems to be thinking how Israel ("God's Child") was liberated from Pharaoh, and not how the Child Jesus returned from the "flight into Egypt." Matthew would probably agree: "That, too!" Behold how the Bible itself quotes the Bible. The same words fit different situations. If it worked for the prophets and evangelists, it can work for us too. So, I retired. Literally, I finished the work You gave me to do. Jesus said that, and it fits me as well.

Priests also retire, nowadays. The current code of canon law (in canon 538 #3) stipulates that a parish priest "upon completing his seventy-fifth year of age" shall submit his resignation from office to the diocesan bishop. After passing the fateful seventy-fifth milestone in early 1999, the present writer dutifully complied with regulations. Anyway, a realistic appraisal of his declining health and energy seemed to indicate he could no longer do a good job at running a large parish. In addition to severe diabetes, he was hospitalized twice in three years with life-threatening ailments: medical conditions that a person could die from, "but they wouldn't let me!" Lord, wasn't that the exit ramp we just passed back there? He seems to smile an enigmatic smile and reply, gently but firmly, "Shut up and drive. OK?"

Then a brilliant young doctor took over, and this priest at eighty is healthier than he was at seventy. Healthy now, and helping out in many more parishes and other places, as one of the Active Reserves. As he paused to count up *how many* places, he came up with about thirty addresses, all within a fifty-mile radius, mostly multiple visits for Masses, confessions, talks. . . . So much for retirement.

The point is, we can never be absolutely sure *when* we will have finished the work that God gave us to do. Still, the night will come eventually. Eventually, all of us will need some short prayer that we can repeat over and over again, as night falls and mind and memory weaken. "Do not cast me off in my old age! In this time of old age, forsake me not!" (Ps.70/71). And finally it will be time for: "Lord Jesus, receive my spirit!"

III

Through many pages, we have been touting the practice of short prayers. Prayers with few words. What if we go one step farther and recommend saying . . . Nothing at all??

Of late, "The Lord and I" have been doing just that in all the many parishes which have called for our services. Urging people to be quiet after receiving Holy Communion, to quit transmitting their own prayers and put themselves in a receiving mode. After all, isn't that what they are supposed to be doing: *receiving the Word?*

21

In normal human relations, part of a polite conversation is to stop talking and listen to the other person. To receive the other person's words. What should we do when it is THE WORD in Person that we are receiving? Shouldn't we suspend even those internal words of ours that we think with, words that we use in talking to ourselves OR in bringing our petitions to the Lord?

All you really have to do is hold still. Be "like a little child on its mother's lap" (Ps. 130/131:2). Mother's, or grandmother's. It would seem that grandmothers are especially good at this kind of thing. Neither she nor the grandchild has to say anything: they just love each other. In the same way, in the loving embrace of Christ the Lord after communion, we don't have to say anything at all. We don't even have to think anything at all, except to think "Jesus" full power. Simply be quiet. Hold still. Yield, and let the Good Lord love you a little. Love you His own way.

This is a prayer, a prayer without words, a prayer of silence. "Be silent in the presence of the Lord God" (Zep. 1:7). Even our official liturgy book recommends an interval of silence after Holy Communion. This is a silence which the mystics of the Middle Ages would well understand.

Someone may point out that Quietism was a heresy. One of the writer's seminary professors liked to say that every heresy is a forgotten dogma. Some truth was being overlooked, neglected, and it got its revenge by coming back and making sure it would be heard. Presenting itself as not only true, but as the whole truth. That wouldn't happen if forgotten truths were allowed to play their proper role. What actually makes a forgotten thesis heretical is when someone exaggerates it, exaggerates something that really needed saying in the first place. It should have been noticed, and kept in proper proportion.

Let's keep this interior post-Communion silence, then, and let's keep it in proper proportion. It is a part of our prayer, and an important part, but not the whole of it. And yet, as time goes by, mindful of the Lord's partiality for short prayers, we might be making our prayers shorter and shorter until at last we are saying nothing at all. If that happens, it won't mean that we have stopped praying. It might only mean that the grace of God in us has finally perfected our process of praying, at long last!

Getting to Know Him

I

As we remarked on an earlier page, this book is not supposed to be about me, but about HIM. Not primarily about the Voice that is the preacher, but rather about the Word Who is being preached. The Word, Who in the homily both speaks and is spoken about.

It turns out that these two aspects of the homily are both of them excellent ways of getting to know Him. Preaching ABOUT Him from the Gospels, and being so CLOSE to Him that He uses your voice to do the preaching. When the Word of God borrows the Voice of a priest to speak to the People, the Voice, for its part, is learning about Christ just as much as the People are. Learning by gaining new insights into the Gospel. Insights that light up the Word-of-God-in-the-book. Light it up from the inside.

The best of the Bible message, the choicest Words-of-God-in-the-book, are to be found in the Gospels. For it is the Gospels that tell us most (even between the lines) about The-Word-of-God-made-flesh-and-dwelling-in-the-midst-of-us. They tell us about Jesus Christ. So lending your voice to the Lord for the purpose of preaching homilies on the Gospel is an excellent way of learning to know Him better. You get more information this way than can be gained by mere study, mere theological lore. While talking WITH Him and talking ABOUT Him, you gain a real familiarity with both Christ AND the Gospels.

II

So, what was He like? REALLY like? First, you have to master the lines of print that tell His story. Tell of His sayings, His ways, His miracles. Notice how differently He interacts with different people. Women, children, sinners, lepers. The grass roots people, the learned, the powerful, the establishment.

Once you are familiar with the text (and many other Scripture texts that intersect with it), you are ready to begin reading *in between* the lines as well as reading on them. You begin to understand WHY He acted the way He did. Eventually, the strong and beautiful Face of "The Christ" will begin to shine up at you from behind the lines of print, almost as if the words of Scripture had been printed on paper that already bore His portrait.

There is, of course, a danger here. If you're not careful, if you're not prayerful, you could end up reading something into the text that was never really there. People have been doing that since Day One. Ascribing to Christ their own ideas and attitudes, often of a kind that He Himself would be the first to repudiate.

We who have met so many well-intentioned (and sometimes not so well-intentioned) Fundamentalists, with their constant refrain of "The Bible says . . . The Bible says . . . ," we may be forgiven for retorting that if these people are rash enough, they can make the Bible say anything they want it to say.

Most of the time, the picture changes radically once you examine the *context* of the text that they are quoting. Often too, it pays to have a look at some other page of the Bible, where you might find an equally inspired text saying just the opposite. Beat your swords into plowshares, if you like to quote Isaiah 2:4. Beat your plowshares into swords, if you prefer to quote Joel 4:10. Finally, let's remember that when tempting Christ, the devil himself was capable of piously quoting Scripture! The devil also knew what "the Bible says." Christ, however, wasn't buying it. He was able to quote the Bible right back, and quote it differently.

III

"What think you of Christ? Whose son is He?" (Mt. 22:42). That always was a most basic question, and it still is. It even took the Church several centuries and several ecumenical councils to get the answer right. The right answer of course is the one contained in the Creeds. In the Nicean Creed, in the Apostles' Creed, and in a still older profession of faith whose framework is still clearly discernible in both. An older profession of faith built around three questions that we still hear at baptisms, and at Easter time. Do you believe in God the Father? In Jesus Christ His only Son our Lord? In the Holy Spirit, the holy Catholic Church . . . ?

It is easy to see how these three questions came to be loosely stitched together with some lesser (though still important) teachings, to form the Apostles' Creed. Christians could then profess their Christian Faith any time, without needing some one to put the questions to them, the way those questions were put to catechumens at baptism.

What concerns us most here is a basic belief "in Jesus Christ, His only Son, our Lord." That was clear enough during the first two centuries and well into the third. Then budding theologians began to qualify this basic truth (the divinity of Christ), not by denying it, but by explaining it. Sort of updating it, putting a more sophisticated spin on it.

You see (claimed the Arians), Christ was not really truly, literally the Son of God by nature—just a creature raised to a quasi-divine status as a reward for holy living. And it came to pass that (to quote an early Christian writer) the world woke up one morning and discovered itself to be Arian. Theological thoughts do seep down to the masses.

Of course, the Holy Spirit would not let them get away with it. An ecumenical council was convened in 325 A.D. at Nicea, near Constantinople, to beef up the Apostles' Creed. Revise it in such a way that there would be no mistake about the real divinity of Jesus

Christ. The result was the Nicean Creed, which we now recite on Sundays.

Most of our church-going Catholics are familiar enough with the existence of two creeds, the Apostles' and the Nicean. However, in all probability, not many of them notice how the former is inside the latter like a skeleton in a body, like a steel framework inside a finished building. They do not reflect on how the baptismal-and-Holy-Saturday "Three Questions" form in turn the skeleton and the framework of the Apostles' Creed. It is good, though, to recognize the continuity of our Christian belief through all three creeds. To see how each statement of faith fits neatly inside the other, how the later ones change nothing in what went before. How they only make that faith more explicit and more clear.

Which is what the assembled Council Fathers did at Nicea in 325 A.D. Arianism had attacked the real divinity of "Jesus Christ His only Son our Lord." Had questioned whether the Lord Jesus was *really* God's Son. It was a line of the creed (Apostles' Creed) that needed emphasizing, and that was the line that got it. "We believe in one Lord, Jesus Christ, the only Son of God . . ." (Add to that: "eternally begotten of the Father"! Because the Arians are claiming that Jesus was just a creature, not "eternally"; and that He was sort of adopted into the Trinity, not "begotten.")

Begotten. Eternally. Got it! What else? Write in that He is "God from God." Well, of course, since He was begotten by the Father, He had to be God from God. . . . Say it anyway! Instead of . . . ? No: in addition to!

All right. Anything else? "Light from Light." OK. What else? "True God from true God." Hombre! We just said that: "God from God . . ." Say it again! And also write in: "begotten, not made." These heretics are saying Jesus was a creature, was created, was something "made." We've got to be unmistakably clear here. But we have that already when we say "eternally begotten of the Father." Well, say it again!

You get the picture. Nicea piled formulation upon formulation to affirm the divinity of Christ—because THAT, after all, was the burning question of the day. The ultimate reason why these bishops were met in council. "What think ye of Christ?" was the question. "Son of God" was their authentic answer, an answer said seven different ways for emphasis.

History repeats itself. Subtly, ever so subtly, the ancient Arian attack on the divinity of Christ slithered its way back into theology. As recently as the period during and immediately after Vatican II, one was always running into some priest or nun or seminarian so eager for aggiornamento, so proud of their boldness and their new sophistication, that they would tell you Christ never claimed to be divine. (Don't tell me it didn't happen! The present writer lived and worked in Rome during those years, and vividly remembers—just for instance—arguing with a priest who was writing for the periodical called *Concilium.* The cutting edge, the latest, the best and the brightest!)

Such proponents of the New Theology considered themselves very progressive and very avant-garde and even very original, though they were actually turning the clock back seventeen centuries to Arian days and Arian errors. Not that they appealed to Arius of Ancient Egypt. Their starting point was rather the demythologizing of Scripture in the fashion then current in Modern Europe. Nevertheless, the finish lines of both groups began to look suspiciously alike.

It was futile trying to argue with these New Breed thinkers of the last quarter of the last century. So you don't think Christ is really divine, really the only-begotten Son of God? "I didn't say that!" Well then, exactly what ARE you saying? "I'm just saying Christ never claimed to be God." What about that scene at the end of John Chapter 8, when the Jews are about to stone Jesus to death for saying "Before Abraham began to be, I AM" (Jn. 8:58). What about Jn. 10:31–33, where they again pick up rocks to stone Him "for blasphemy, because you, mere man though you are, are making yourself out to be God?" What about Mt. 26:63–66; If you don't want to accept John, what about the high priest questioning Jesus to say under oath whether He is the Son of God? The whole Sanhedrin understood His answer to be a clear and solemn "yes"—blasphemy, in their book.

All of these people were contemporaries of Jesus, all of them heard Him talking in His and their own mother tongue, which they understood better than any modern exegete. They knew well enough what His words and expressions meant. And they understood Him to be saying that He was every bit as divine as Yahweh, the One True God was divine.

"Well, the Gospels were written so much later. Especially John. We don't know what Jesus REALLY said, what REALLY happened at his trial. The Gospel accounts reflect the Easter faith of the Christian community, the way things were worded several generations later." Thanks, my friend! If you think you can face the Lord with this sort of reasoning when life is over, that's up to you. For my part, I think I will stay with the mainstream Christian community of then and of now. Accepting the Gospels and the early councils as we have them: now that makes a lot more sense to me.

Well, at what point did Jesus realize that He was more than just human? Before we tackle a question like this, we ought to acknowledge that we may never know the answer, and that in all probability we would not be able to understand it even if it were given to us. After all, only ONE person ever had the experience of operating on these two levels, the divine and the human. To understand how it would be possible for Jesus in His real humanity to know or to be ignorant of something that He (the same divine person!) had to know full well by reason of His divinity. . . . To understand how that worked, you would have to be both human-and-divine yourself. Some things will always remain beyond our ken, and we might as well admit it.

Nevertheless, bearing this caveat in mind, we could make a suggestion. Let's be such mavericks that we will accept (in spite of

29

some learned reservations about it) Luke's first two chapters as being the things that Mary the Mother of Jesus kept in her heart, reflecting on them through the years (Lk. 2:19) until Luke showed up and interviewed *her* as one of the prime "eyewitnesses" mentioned in his own Gospel (Lk. 1:2–3). This, by the way, is Luke's Gospel as we have it, not just a pious writer of bygone days whom moderns no longer believe, someone whom "nobody" quotes anymore.

So, we accept Mary's memories of the time when Jesus was twelve years old. How He stayed behind in the temple without first getting permission, without saying anything at all about it (Lk. 2:42–46). When his mother pointed out that they had been looking all over for Him, He gave her this enigmatic answer (v. 49): "Didn't you realize I'd be here, in My Father's house?" Despite a few paraphrastic translations like, "My Father's business" (King James and Douay), or Father's "affairs" (Jerusalem Bible), the plain meaning of His words was His Father's house, His Father's property, as in most extant English versions. So: "When you go looking for someone's son, what more natural place for him to be than in his father's house?" The temple was "the House of God." If this temple, where they found Him, was His "Father's House," then God was His Father. And He knew it with perfect clarity at the age of twelve. Knew that this was where He belonged. Knew that He was the Son of God.

IV

So we accept it as fully true, that Jesus Christ was (and IS) the Son of God. That is true; but that is not the whole truth. One hundred percent true, but not one hundred percent of the truth. The other half of the equation, which must always be borne in mind with equal clarity, is this: Christ was (and is) the Son of Man. In fact, that is what He called Himself by preference: the Son of Man.

It was almost like He wanted to stress the fact that He was thoroughly human, and proud of it.

THOROUGHLY human? Yes, and thoroughly divine. Our own mental horizon is too narrow to take in both of these tremendous truths at once, to keep both "natures" in mind at the same time, Because of this "narrow-mindedness," we tend to focus on either the divine nature or the human, concentrating on that one nature and, at best, holding the other one at the edge or periphery of our mental field of vision. It probably can't be helped. However, we can at least keep reminding ourselves that Christ is not half-god and half-man, that He is wholly divine and wholly human. How that works, how it's possible, we'll probably never know. It's a good thing we are only required to believe it, not required to understand it.

That said, half a century of preaching Christ, of getting to know Him from close up, has brought about a certain subtle change in the mind of this particular priest. A change in how he sees Christ nowadays, compared with the way he felt about Christ during seminary years and earlier. At first, his focus was almost entirely on the divine. As time went by, he became increasingly fascinated with the human "side" of the Lord as well. Full awareness that Christ is God, and hence in a class by Himself, has not thereby been diminished in the least. There has only been a tremendous increase in his awareness of how delightfully *human* Christ is besides. It even seems (paradoxically enough) that only God could have done such a beautiful job of becoming human.

Human enough to like some people more than others. He hand-picked His twelve closest collaborators, but among them there was an inner circle of three: Peter, James, and John. (Why was Andrew left out? After all, he had come on board before his brother Simon-Peter. Had even recruited him.) Nonetheless, when Christ felt like taking along certain close intimates, to the heights of Tabor or the inner recesses of Gethsemani, they were three in number; not four, not twelve. Of the three, John was a clear favorite. John, who missed no opportunity of mentioning the fact that He WAS Jesus' favorite. The Disciple Whom Jesus Loved (and proud of it!).

Sorry, John. I had to get that "dig" in. You won't mind. . . . Your privileged place in the heart of Christ is something we sort of envy you for. Jealous. But at the same time, it gives us grounds to hope that He Who does indeed play favorites, may somehow make a favorite of us as well! To a lesser degree than yourself, surely. But just as really . . .

Humanly, too, Christ had other special friends. "He 'loved' Martha and her sister and Lazarus" (Jn. 11:5). We read how Christ wanted, how He needed, the human companionship of His closest disciples on the night when He underwent His agony in the garden (Mt. 26:38). Christ is no stranger to human feelings, to human emotions.

His heart is moved with pity for the widow of Naim, who is weeping over the loss of her only son. "Don't cry!" He says. And for her, He works a miracle (Lk. 7:11–15).

He hugs (literal translation!) little children (Mk. 10:16), and gets upset with His well-meaning Apostles for trying to shoo them away. More than once, He gets humanly exasperated when these same thick-headed disciples are so slow about catching on (Mt. 16:5–12 and Mt. 16:23).

One time, when a certain man requests a miracle of healing for his son, Jesus sounds rather annoyed, is even disgusted "because you people don't want to believe unless you see miracles" (Jn. 4:46–50). Some people, like the scribes, did not want to believe even when they DID see miracles. With them He was downright angry for their stubbornness, for resisting grace as they did. Humanly angry, and He did not mince words about it either (Mk. 3:5; Lk. 11:39–52).

Tired and thirsty and worn out from walking in the summer's heat, the human Lord sits down to rest by the well of Jacob, while His disciples trek on into town to buy provisions (John, Chapter

32

4). He is thirsty enough, and human enough, to break the taboos of His time and place: He starts a conversation with a woman, and a Samaritan woman at that! Much to her surprise, and that of His disciples when they return from town and find Him talking to her. There is more: Jesus is so thirsty that He is even willing to break the strong taboo that forbade Him to drink from her heretical water jar!

Surprised she certainly was, and not overly friendly. Jesus, however, does not get personally upset and reply to her in kind. Instead, He seems to be teasing her when He says, "Hey! If you only knew who I am, you'd be the one asking Me for water." For living water (= running water).

He plays on her curiosity, her self-interest. Intrigued by the idea of running water in her own kitchen, the Samaritan Lady thinks (and says): Let's have it!

Tongue in cheek, the Savior suggests, "Why don't you call your husband, and we'll talk about it?" Sensitive issue! "I am not married," says the lady, crisply, intending to close that topic. Don't go there!

Still teasing, Jesus retorts: "You said it, you're not married. You're not married to that guy you're now living with, for instance; and you were not married to any of the five that came before him either. No, married you are not!"

Embarrassed now, and realizing that she has been maneuvered onto dangerous ground, the woman hastily attempts to change the subject. "Oh, if you know THAT, then you must be a prophet. So what do you as a prophet have to say about these two rival temples . . . ?"

The disciples return from town with the food they purchased, and they are surprised to find Jesus talking to a *woman.* And a Samaritan one at that! The Lord often surprises even His closest co-workers. For them it's always a chance to learn more about Him, to get to know Him even better.

Imagine the surprise of good Mass-going Catholics if they

were to catch their pastor on the front steps of their parish church, not only *talking to* "that kind of woman," but even *joking* about her notorious marital status! Someone would surely write a letter to the bishop. The pastor's plain duty would be to rebuke such a person. But to make jokes and tease her about her immoral lifestyle, instead of denouncing it? Scandalous! What's the Church coming to, anyway?

We can be grateful to St. John the Evangelist (AND to the Holy Spirit as well!) for preserving evidence that Christ the Lord possessed a fine sense of humor—along with other precious human qualities. Jesting with the Lady of Samaria in chapter four is only one instance. There is another instance in chapter eight, just a few pages later, in the midst of a very serious matter involving a woman caught in the act of adultery. The one that the good law-abiding people are all set to lynch, in retribution for her sinful act and in obedience to the Law of Moses. "The Bible says . . ." (What about the man? There had to be a man involved in her act of adultery. Takes two to tango, you know! The way such things go, he may even have been the one who initiated their affair. So does he get punished too? No? Why not?)

All the world now knows how the Lord Jesus was shrewd enough to save the woman, and still avoid His opponents' trap. At least, people know the bottom line about casting the first stone, even if they are vague about how that line came to be pronounced. Do they notice how Jesus thereby avoids contradicting "Moses and the Law" (though He did that on other occasions)? He simply places a condition that renders the penalty inoperative. He simply specifies who it is that shall have the honor of throwing the first stone (not all of them, just the first!). All the while He knows full well that He is the only person who would qualify. And He knows He isn't throwing any stones: not that day, not ever.

So He is merciful; He is forgiving. No zero tolerance here. But where is the sense of humor that we claimed to find in this chapter? It is implied in His question, in His mock surprise at finding Himself all alone with the sinner because all her would-be executioners had had to slink away one by one. "Why, where did everybody go?" He could hardly have said that without smiling in His beard at their comic retreat.

If He smiled at this scene, serious as it was, He must have laughed right out loud when the Lady from Lebanon bested Him in His own argument. (Remember? The Lady who wouldn't take "no" for an answer!) "O Woman! Great is thy faith! Let it be done!" Christ the Lord could appreciate a bon mot when He heard one; He also knew how to give in gracefully when the situation demanded it. You've got to love a Leader like that!

You've also got to love a Leader who—like the Lord—knows when to make an exception. We don't mean that superior officers and religious superiors have to do it ALL the time. That might simply indicate that they themselves are basically undisciplined, that they will yield to pressure from any subordinate. Rather, the ideal is the sort of superior who in his own life can echo the words of the Lord, "I always do what My Father wants" (Jn. 8:29); and yet understands when it is time to make an exception for the "little guy."

We admire the Lord for His resolute single-mindedness about obeying the will of His Father (Jn. 8:29 and Gethsemani). That same faithfulness to His Father's "game plan" moved Him to protest to His own mother at Cana of Galilee that His hour "had not yet come!" (Jn. 2:4). Later, when He and the disciples were enjoying a day off down at the coast, He explained to them why He wasn't working any miracles for Lebanese Ladies: He had been "sent only to the lost sheep of the House of Israel" (Mt. 15:24).

With all due respect, Lord! Wouldn't it seem that Your hour still had not yet come just a few minutes later, when You had the waiters fill the stone jars with water, and turned that water into wine? And what about the Lebanese Lady (the one who wouldn't take "no" for an answer)? If she was not one of the lost sheep of the House of Israel when she cried after you on the street, then she still wasn't one a couple minutes later when You worked a miracle for her anyway. At least twice You bent the rules; at least on two occasions You went outside the parameters of Your mission. We are grateful for the lesson. But more important: You look more human, more likeable, more "follow-able" for being like that.

Observing You closely, we have to conclude that for all Your dedication to your Father's will, You knew when and how to bend the rules just a little bit, for the good of others! Not always, not in every case, but without scruples when the situation called for it. That alone makes You more human than most of the humans who wield some authority in Church or State. Even some parents of teen-age children might profit by taking You as a model.

In these days of a "zero tolerance" policy adopted by Church Leaders, no one is quoting the Gospel nor looking for any guidelines there. We wonder, though, if You Who gave us the line about the millstone did not also want bishops to consider Your mercy to a poor woman whom the Law was about to lynch. "Go, and sin no more," You told her. Isn't that what some bishops were saying to some sinners in the years that now provoke people's righteous indignation?

You also gave us a parable about good and bad fish together in the same net, mingled until the final sorting-out that will take place at the shore (not over deep water). You told us another about the Enemy sowing thistles among the wheat, and how the wise landowner did not want eager-beaver farm hands to go stomping out into the field to uproot the thistles (and trample a lot of good wheat in the process).

Odd, isn't it, how our media-driven era with its million-dollar-settlements can get so surprised and so outraged, and even have their faith shaken, when things turn out exactly as You predicted that they would? When bad fish are found in the net and thistles in the wheatfield, that ought to increase people's faith. "By crackey! The Lord really called that one. It all turned out exactly as He said it would!" Instead, many seem to feel that they have reason to lose faith in You, and certainly have nothing to do anymore with the kind of net and the kind of wheatfield where not everyone is as pure and holy as they themselves are (not)!

Your blood was to be shed—and You knew it—so that sins might be forgiven. Where forgiveness is excluded, so is Your spirit. Sinners flocked to You because of that spirit, Lord, and I have a feeling they always will. And that good people will always condemn them, in our century as they did back then, in Your time.

People sin because they are human. According to Heb. 2:17, this was why You became human, became one of us so that we would have a merciful High Priest, one able to understand and expiate our sins. You became human in order to carry our burden of guilt for us, to atone for it. Perhaps in order to experience first-hand the limitations of being human.

In the comic strip "Peanuts" (which I am sure You would have enjoyed at Nazareth), the little boy named Linus once avowed that: "I do so love humanity! It's *people* that I can't stand!" One suspects that there are a great many who unconsciously share his sentiments. But some of us at least are glad that You, our High Priest, are not like that. You love humanity in the abstract (which is relatively easy to do), but you also loved concrete real-life people (which can get rather difficult at times). Your love for ordinary sinful people was a scandal to the Scribes and Pharisees (Lk. 15:2), to whom You pointed out that they might as well criticize doctors for being around sick people so much of the time (Lk. 5:31).

It's really great having a High Priest like YOU! One able to sympathize with our weakness because You have "been there" yourself. You scoped out the territory that we need to cover, You personally tested our human limitations. Just noticing that about You generates a great deal of confidence in us: the conviction that we, too, will find help and mercy and forgiveness when we need it (Heb. 4:15–16). Not "if" we ever need it, but "when" we will.

Christ is so like us, even while He is and remains so far superior to us. Here is a Leader with Whom we can identify. One we can love and serve and follow. What a privilege it is to serve Him and to service *with* Him, to work together so closely with this divine (so divine!) and human (so very human!) Christ. Contemplating Him, we can only conclude that God becoming human (the Incarnation) was a truly great idea!

I wonder if we will ever get back to an era when church bells will ring out three times a day (6–12–6), in order to remind us of the Incarnation? We can never thank God too much nor too often that "the Word WAS made flesh, and that He dwelt amongst us"!

What He Actually Said Was . . .

When you are trying, really trying, to lend your voice to the Lord Christ, so that He may use it to continue His own preaching of the word, there is often a flash of new insight that lights up a given Gospel text from the inside.

We said that already. The question might be asked, for whom will such a Gospel passage be lighted up? For the Voice, certainly. Also for the people who are attentively listening to the Voice, who are actually listening to the Word all unawares. The Word, Who still uses a human voice "to teach them many things" (Mk. 6:34). Again and again, in many different parishes, someone stops the preacher (the Voice) after Mass and says, "I never realized what that text meant. But it's so clear!"

There is, of course, no guarantee that the same insight will seem equally clear to everyone. Especially those who were not there listening to the Word. The new insight might even be rejected by some persons whose academic training has prepared them to teach Scripture or theology professionally.

Why? Because our educational system conditions us to accept new ideas and interpretations, not even from "the Church," but solely from the Approved Authors. That is, only from books and articles written by certain scholars, academics who have been recognized by "the establishment" of their peers. No matter how clear and sensible an explanation may be, unless it derives from such a source (properly documented by footnotes), it is in danger of being rejected. Not because it is impossible or wrong; not because it has been "condemned by the Church" (nowadays few theologians are), but simply because "I keep up with the literature on this matter, and nowhere have I read what you are suggesting."

The literature, in turn, is heavily guarded by editors who decide what is and what is not worth printing in the journals they manage. Inevitably, current fashion has a great influence on their decision. Which big-name university counts the would-be writer among its faculty members? Back in the 1930s and 1940s, when the present writer first explored the Catholic academic world, the scene was dominated by people like Billot, Garrigou-LaGrange, and (in philosophy) Jacques Maritain. (And . . . where is THAT in the Summa???) During Vatican II and immediately after, nothing ever got published without quoting Karl Rahner.

It was probably to counteract such a closed mentality in the schools (the universities) of his own time that the writer of *The Imitation* advised his readers: "Ask not WHO said it; rather, pay attention to WHAT is being said" (I, 5). That is good advice. Not everything that has been written is true. On the other hand, not everything that is true has been written, either.

II

In our search for what the Gospels are really saying, we soon learn not to put too much faith in any particular translation. Especially English translations. A wild welter of them has appeared in the past seventy years, and what we now have is truly a mixed bag. Time was, when the English-language field was dominated by the King James Version for Protestants and the Douay-Rheims-Challoner Bible for Catholics. Then the dike burst. A flood of English versions inundated our biblical landscape. This writer has a full dozen different English Bibles on his own bookshelf, and he probably doesn't have them all. Their quality varies widely. None of them can even claim to be an adequate substitute for reading the Greek (or even the Latin Vulgate) text.

It is true that sometimes a translation into some modern id-iom—not necessarily English, but not excluding it either—can prove to be a real help. The Word can make use of such Voices also to shed new light on an old text. Nonetheless, a decent acquaintance with the Greek text of the Gospels is indispensable. Personally, we rely on the Greek New Testaments edited by Merk and Nestle-Aland.

As for other Scripture scholars, we do not simply write them off nor do we spurn the insights that they have to offer. We are aware that the Word can speak through them, too. Many moderns did succumb to the reigning Bultmania which tyrannized the last century; but others (both in our camp and out of it) were as good as it gets. American Catholics in particular can point proudly to *The Jerome Biblical Commentary* and the many towering intellects that stood behind it. Particularly the late Raymond Brown, whose work entitled, *An Introduction to the New Testament* is a monument of sanity as well as of scholarship. A new series is now focusing on what ancient Christian commentators had to say about the Scriptures. Nevertheless . . . no commentator can ever replace the reading of the original texts.

For that, so far as the New Testament is concerned, one has to be able to work with an unabridged dictionary like *Liddell & Scott's Greek-English Lexicon,* out of Oxford. Or better, the huge multivolume *Theological Dictionary of the New Testament*, edited first in German by Kittel and Friedrich and now available in English. And a concordance: because the Bible itself, on its other pages, is often the very best tool for interpreting a vexing Bible passage.

So scholars do help? Undoubtedly. But they are not infallible. They must all yield to the word-of-God-in-the-book: to what is indicated by the text and context. Especially, they must all yield to the Word in Person. And He is no one's captive, however learned or however holy a scholar might be.

III

Seeing a text in a new light brings with it a thrill of discovery, an "a-ha! Erlebnis" as a German philosopher called it. That doesn't mean no one ever thought of this new insight before, but as a rule it does mean that there has been a general agreement to understand a particular text in a certain locked-in way. A way that both we and everybody else seems to have gotten used to.

For example, what did Jesus really say in Jn. 14:6? Many versions, and the majority of the people who quote from them, have Jesus professing Himself to be THREE distinct things: the WAY and the TRUTH and the LIFE. All on an equal plane of discourse. Paragraph One, Paragraph Two, Paragraph Three.

Both the Greek and the Latin can indeed be translated that way. Three separate independent nouns connected by conjunctions, "et" (or kai) meaning "and". However, an equally good translation could take that "et . . . et" or "kai . . . kai" as a "both . . . and," enclosing "the Truth" and "the Life" into one doublet. Together, the Truth-and-Life duo (T/L) then explains HOW Jesus is "the Way".

How are we going to read Jn. 14:6 then? "The Way AND the Truth AND the Life"? As almost everybody quotes it? Or should we maybe punctuate it like this: "I am the WAY—(that is, I am) the Truth and the Life"? Or: "I am the Way: the Truth and the Life." In olden times, manuscripts and scribes did not use dashes or colons. If they had, the Evangelist might have used one or the other of them here. Because if we examine the context, it was "the Way" that was under discussion. One topic, not three.

Read the verse in the whole context of John, Chapter 14. What were they talking about? How did this come up? Jesus says, you know the way that leads where I am going. Thomas protests that we can't possibly know which road to take until we first find out where You are going—and that is something we do NOT know. To which the Lord Jesus retorts, "I am the Way." You don't know the Way? After all this time—as He says to Philip in this same chapter—you still don't know ME?

Thomas said, "We DON'T know 'the Way' "; and Jesus said, "I AM the Way." Poor Thomas! A no-nonsense, both-feet-on-the-ground sort of guy, with little use for figurative language (like: "Lazarus is asleep" Jn. 11:11–16). Thomas doesn't see how any person, even the Master Himself, can be a "way." A way is a path, a road. . . .

So Christ spells it out for him. For him, and for us. "I am the WAY, (because I am) the Truth and the Life." The context makes this meaning clear, and to their credit, several translations have recognized the fact. The Jerusalem Bible, the New English, the King James, the New International, the Revised English Bible. Admittedly, no one is going to be led astray by our NAB and by the Revised Standard Version, which choose the Way AND the Truth AND the Life alternative; but they do miss the point. Just as people miss the point when they misquote Lincoln's Gettysburg Address about "government OF the people, BY the people, FOR the people . . ." as three parallel elements. ALL government is a governing OF the people. What is special is, when this governing of them is done BY them and is done FOR them.

IV

Another passage where the context is key to the meaning is in the conversation between Christ and Nicodemus in John, Chapter Three. Is it "born again"? Or "born FROM ABOVE"?

Here in Jn. 3:3, both the Jerusalem Bible and our official NAB opt for "born from above." This is a minority opinion. Most English translations have "born AGAIN." We wonder whether JB and NAB might perhaps have been influenced by a rather shaky argument in the prestigious (and otherwise excellent) *Theological Dictionary of the New Testament,* vol. I, page 378.

The NAB's explanatory note to Jn 3:3 is this: Jesus was saying "from above," while Nicodemus was understanding "again." Such a misunderstanding might possibly be plausible had the two been speaking Greek, where "anothen" may indeed have either meaning. However, in all likelihood, Jesus and Nicodemus would have been conversing in Aramaic or perhaps Hebrew. Judging from his reaction, Nicodemus evidently understood Jesus to be saying, "you need to be born again." So from the context, we can conclude that this is what Jesus really said: "born again."

What did He mean by it? Accustomed as we are to hearing "born again Christians" use the term, we unconsciously ascribe the same meaning to the words of Jesus. However, judging again from the context, we find Him explaining to Nicodemus that this rebirth would be achieved "by water and the Spirit." By baptism.

In contrast, contemporary "born agains" are talking about a conversion experience. Nothing un-biblical about that, of course. Except that the Greek Scriptures use other terms for it, like metanoia and cognates, which mean someone had a "change of heart." (Not like a confrere whose first language was German: preaching a women's Day of Recollection in unfamiliar English, he encouraged the ladies to have a "change of life.")

Conversion is a biblical imperative. It came out strongly in the preaching of Jesus, as in the preaching of John the Baptist before Him. "Repent! Believe! For the kingdom of heaven is at hand!" (Mk. 1:15; Mt. 3:2 and 4:17). It also occurs in preaching found in the Acts. So it is biblical: but it's not based on "born again," Jn. 3.

V

When Jesus was a guest in the home of Martha, what did He say to her, in Lk 10:41–42? Comparing ten English translations, and reflecting on the Master as we know Him from the whole of the Gospel record, it would seem that Phillips Modern English comes closest with: "You are bothered about PROVIDING SO MANY THINGS. Only ONE THING is really needed." (Even that wording is going to need some explaining!)

The worst choice of words seems to be that of the New English Bible, which has Jesus telling Martha that she is "fretting and fussing about so many things." Let's remember that "Jesus loved Martha" (Jn. 11:5). One doubts that He would be so rude as to insult His good-friend-and-hostess by calling her a fuss-budget. Especially when she was knocking herself out trying to prepare a nice meal for Him. (Wouldn't that reduce any woman to tears!)

Perhaps our interpretation is obvious, since it neatly fits almost anyone's translation, as well as the original text. Martha was so fond of Jesus, so eager to please Him with the finest products of her culinary skill, that she left herself (and Him!) no time to just sit down and talk and listen—the way her sister Mary was doing at the feet of Christ. Martha complains that Mary isn't helping. Jesus tells her very kindly that He would be satisfied with just ONE dish (think: just a plate of pasta in Italy, or just a plate of boiled rice in the Philippines). Only ONE THING is necessary = "All we really need is ONE DISH." So you can sit down and talk too.

It is true that masters (and mistresses) of the spiritual life have long seen in the words of Jesus a lofty reference to the contemplative life, "the one thing necessary," so far superior to the active life. We respect their opinion. In offering this, our more pedestrian interpretation of Jesus' words, we remember that the sayings of Holy Writ can have multiple meanings, as observed above ("Out of Egypt I called My Son . . .").

In a very real sense it is true that paying attention to God and to Christ is the most important thing, is all that really matters in the long run. "Seek ye first the kingdom of God, and all the rest will be thrown into the bargain" (Mt. 6:33). On the other hand, Christ Himself saw that people's stomachs needed bread, even while their minds were being filled with the Truth of God. "These people have been with Me for three days," He says, "and they have nothing to eat. I do not want to send them on their way fasting, lest they faint along the road" (Mt. 15:32, Mk. 8:2–3). Would our devout Christian ascetics have dared to remind the Lord, "You Yourself said that only one thing is necessary: spiritual food, not the bodily kind. Let them eat truth. That's all that matters."

Once again, it seems to be a case of "both/and" meanings rather than an "either/or." The "one thing necessary" (= all we really need) could and did refer very concretely to ONE DISH, one plate, at an actual physical meal in Martha's home. It can ALSO have an allegorical meaning, the kind of contemplative spiritual food that Mary was taking in that day at the feet of Christ. Because even in the Gospel setting (could we call THAT a *Sitz im Leben*?) . . . even in our reading of "one dish is all we need," Christ clearly would rather have our attention than our service.

VI

There is probably much more at stake in interpreting Mt. 5:28—the well-known line about looking lustfully at a woman and thereby committing adultery with her in one's heart. The problem here is not so much in translating the few simple words, but in deciding what they really mean *in this context.*

This passage has been cited by many moral theologians and other Christian writers-preachers as a proof that unchaste thoughts are, in and of and by themselves, *ex toto genere gravi.* Meaning that they are gravely sinful if consciously and willfully indulged in.

Now, it is one thing to ascertain a possible consensus of mainstream authors, whose opinion could be demonstrated by their having used this text as a proof. It is quite another matter to argue from this text as if it WERE a proof: as if it were a clear Bible proof that such thoughts are *gravely* sinful by their very nature.

Whether or when there ever was such a consensus among moral theologians would be a study all by itself. It is interesting that the new and official Catechism of the Catholic Church cites Mt. 5:28 at least five times (nos. 1456, 2336, 2380, prior-to-2514, 2528) without ever once using it as a proof for the *gravity* of such thoughts.

As in all other cases when some conclusion is being drawn from a Gospel text, it is important to view that text in its *context*. Not to rip it out of its scriptural surroundings and view it in isolation. So what is the context here?

In this part of the Sermon on the Mount, Jesus is represented as contrasting His teaching with the Old Law. Specifically and all in a row, this is done with three of the Ten Commandments: against adultery, killing, and swearing falsely. He emphasizes that His intent is to "fulfill" the Mosaic Law, not do away with it (Mt. 5:17).

(The part about "not one jot or tittle being abolished" [Mt. 5:18)] is difficult to reconcile with the changes He Himself made in the case of divorce [Mt. 19:8–9; Mk. 10:5–9] and in the case of unclean foods [Mk. 7:19]. The present writer has no satisfactory solution to this problem: but that doesn't mean there isn't any.)

In the setting of the Sermon on the Mount, however, His declared intent is to "fulfill" the Law of Moses, to perfect it, tighten it up, hone it to a finer edge. The Catechism justly observes (n. 2336) that Jesus "interprets God's plan strictly" in the Sermon on the Mount. Using our modern idiom, He'd be telling us, "Do not sin? Murder, adultery, perjury? I say, don't even *think* about it!"

Which is **not at all** the same as saying that a lustful look is "**just as bad as**" actually doing it. Common sense alone would convince us that the actual carrying out of a rape or adultery or seduction is worse (a lot worse!) than just entertaining a temptation to do it. In the case of the sixth commandment (no adultery) as in the case of the fifth (no murder), Christ is telling us to avoid what could be the first step leading up to the actual deed. That by no means implies that such a first step is **equivalent** to going all the way. Without trivializing such "first steps," we need not conclude that they are "just as bad as" the ultimate ones and those that lie in between.

As already observed, the context is important in shedding light on this teaching of Christ about "thou shalt not commit adultery." There is perfect symmetry, a perfect parallel, between what is here said of the sixth commandment and what is said right next to it in the very same chapter about the fifth (Mt. 5:21–22). And then in Mt. 5:33–37, about oaths and the eighth commandment. (Eighth, or second. In researching oaths and mental reservation in early manuals of moral theology [1500s, Gregorian University, Rome], the present writer remembers being surprised that those authors treated the matter under the second commandment, about not taking the name of God in vain. That is, taking it falsely.)

Perjury, swearing falsely, is gravely sinful according to our moral theologians. Yet none of them would argue, on the basis of the Sermon on the Mount (Mt. 5:34ff), that even a truthful oath must be gravely sinful; after all, the Lord explicitly says here not to swear at all. Such a conclusion has indeed been drawn by many of our contemporaries; but it goes back at least far enough to have been expressly condemned by the Council of Constance in the 1400s. With reason. For centuries, Christian feudal society was based on oaths of allegiance and fealty. In certain circumstances, the Church herself required her children to take oaths, and still does.

No killing, no anger. No adultery, no lustful looks. No perjury, no oaths at all. If any of our people want to argue that "the Lord said lustful looks are adultery," would they be consistent enough to say that being angry is murder, or that any oath at all is perjury? After all, the Lord does condemn true oaths and false ones in the same breath. If it be ridiculous to read Him this way, so is the argument that any lustful thought is mortally sinful just because adultery is.

Oaths of any kind are comparatively rare, but anger is not. And in the Sermon on the Mount, the section on murder/anger is perfectly parallel to the sections on adultery and oaths. It was laid down in the Old Law that anyone who killed would be liable to judgment (Mt. 5:21). In the New Law being promulgated by Jesus, the same penalty ("liable to judgment") is prescribed for being angry with one's brother. Now, killing one's neighbor is (usually anyway!) regarded as a mortal sin. Does this mean that in the New Law, getting angry at one's neighbor (or at one's children?) is mortally sinful as well? To entertain a fantasy about murdering some obnoxious individual might arguably be regarded as sinful. But *gravely* sinful, if it is not acted upon? Is being angry with someone "just as bad" as actually slaying them? Remember: the New Law prescribes the same penalty for anger that the Old Law prescribed for murder!

To sum up: What did Jesus *really* say in Mt. 5:28? Personally, we can no longer believe that He was presenting unchaste thoughts as the moral equivalent of unchaste deeds. True, the thought alone is not praiseworthy; it is in the same direction as the deed; it could in some cases (though not usually) be a first step towards the deed, as it was for David with the wife of Uriah. But that is by no means the same as ascribing equal malice to the deed and the thought; not tantamount to saying the one is "just as bad" as the other. Perhaps on other grounds, it might still be possible to argue that unchaste or lustful thoughts are "ex toto genere" mortal. However, you can't use Mt. 5:28 as a scriptural proof, nor claim that this is what Jesus really said.

VII

The foregoing discussion suggests another question: What is the relative importance of sexual morality in the whole Christian scheme of things? On Christ's list of priorities, and on our own?

Let there be no mistake about where this discussion is coming from, nor about where it is going. We are NOT saying that the misuse of human sexuality is no sin. We are not implying that it is no big deal. The issue is rather, exactly where does this type of sin rank among all sins? Has it perhaps received more attention than it really deserves? More importance than Christ Himself gave it?

Looking back from the vantage point of his eighty-first year, this writer feels that he was blessed with a good orthodox Catholic education during the "First Quarter" of his life and well into the Second. An excellent, thorough seminary training, preceded by Catholic schools both elementary and secondary, as well as good priests and good confessors in good practicing parishes. That said, it is a bit surprising to realize only now, in the "Fourth Quarter" of life, how much attention and how much zeal those dedicated teachers of the Catholic religion were devoting to "holy purity." That seemed to get the most stress: even to the detriment of faith, forgiveness, or the love of God and neighbor. ("Also rans?")

Though our teachers never actually said so in so many words, some of us (at least some) got the idea that chastity was really the First and Greatest Commandment. Certainly, it was the one you had to worry about most, so far as your eternal salvation was concerned. For this was the big sin-or-virtue on which your judgment would depend at the end of life. Had the question of ranking ever come up, it might have been hard to explain to us boys why this was the Sixth Commandment and not the First.

And then one summer's day in the 1980s, when this one Missouri boy had grown up to be a Country Pastor in Texas, he happened to be preaching a brief homily on a weekday Gospel. One that told of the Lord's warning: how the sinners of Sodom would be getting off easier on Judgment Day than would certain Holy Land towns, the towns that would not accept the preaching of the Faith by His Apostles (Mt. 10:15; Lk. 10:12).

Now Sodom, as everyone knows, was notorious for a particularly gross sexual sin that has gone by the name of that town ever since. Was there really something worse in the eyes of the Lord? Some sin, any sin, that had nothing whatever to do with passion or with sex, but "only" (!) with faith vs. indifference? Those more wicked towns did not even persecute the messengers of the Gospel—they "only" ignored them. Resisted grace, rejected the Lord's offer of salvation, refused to believe. Evidently—thought the priest—the priorities of Christ the Lord must be radically different from ours.

Not long after the "Sodom Sermon," and quite independently of the same, the Country Pastor was preparing for publication a manuscript which involved Gospel teaching on marriage and sex. In sifting through the Gospels with an eye out for this, the Country Pastor was surprised to notice for the first time how little the Lord had to say on this subject at all.

A subject which (as observed above) had loomed so large in his catechism studies and seminary training. Our "morals" textbook in the seminary came in four fat volumes, one for each of the four years of theology. One volume each for Principles of Morality, for Commandments, for Sacraments, and . . . for Sex. Volume IV was entirely dedicated to spelling out every sexual sin that a person could possibly commit, and quite a few that, at the time, seemed downright impossible for anyone to commit at all.

Now, if it took one whole volume out of four to cover the subject of "sex" in our seminary studies, a whole one-fourth of our "moral theology"course, one might reasonably expect that this same awful topic would occupy at least one fourth of the Gospel pages. It doesn't. Jesus has a good deal to say to the Pharisees about their hypocrisy, a great deal to say about faith and forgiveness. But He has very little to say about sex. And even that "little" seems mostly concerned with adultery (He didn't like it). Moreover, when confronted with real-life sexual sinners, Christ did not seem overly concerned whether someone might be a prostitute (see Lk. 7:39), or whether she might have had half-a-dozen live-in

51

boy friends (Jn. 4:18). As for masturbation, premarital sex . . . Not a single word.

OK: so there ARE some remarks in the epistles about such matters; and that is Scripture too. But it is not in the Gospels, and it is not something that we hear directly from the Lord. Something that He considered important enough to fulminate against. Which might well suggest that sex and chastity and the sixth commandment (except for adultery!) were not nearly so important in the eyes of Christ as they subsequently became in the eyes of our Christian teachers. Without going to the other extreme (of undue laxity), perhaps we Christians ought to re-think our own priorities, and worry a bit more about some things that seem to have "worried" Christ a bit more. If our list of more serious sins does not agree with His, then somebody is mistaken. And it is not Him!

*   *   *

These are a few examples of seeing old familiar texts in context, seeing them in a new and unfamiliar light. Thinking about them, thinking them through, should help us toward a sounder understanding of Christian living. Even more important: we may end up understanding Christ better.

Liturgy—Serving God and Community

The first (and perhaps the most important) document produced by Vatican II was the Constitution on the Sacred Liturgy.

From the very beginning of the first Council session, "the Liturgy" became a test case and a battle ground between "The Curia"—seen as entrenched in the City on the Tiber—and the opposed attacking forces of local churches located roughly along the Rhein River (in Holland, Belgium, Germany, and France). The present writer has vivid personal memories of those times, having arrived in Rome to stay in 1964, when Council Fever was at its height.

Before that, during seminary days in the 1940s, liturgy loomed large in his priestly training. Not so much in the classroom as outside of it. In the majestic seminary chapel with its oversized sanctuary and its super-solemn ceremonies, where we offered frequent High Masses, sang weekend Vespers and Compline, and enjoyed the grandest possible celebrations of all high feasts. Those were the times when Latin texts from the Vulgate sang their way into our memories, borne on the wings of haunting melodies from age-old Gregorian chants.

In a sense, our outfit was on the cutting edge, an unconscious forerunner of Vatican II. It is true that Liturgy as a classroom subject did not rank with the Big Kids—Dogma, Morals, Exegesis, and Canon Law. Worse: the afternoon slot that Liturgy occupied, right after lunch and outdoor physical recreation, often turned it into a veritable "lethargy class."

However, in many other ways more practical than academic,

we were made familiar with Dom Gueranger, Pius Partsch, Beuron and Maria Laach. . . . In short, we were exposed to the same influences that formed the Rhein River People, those same people who went to Rome for Vatican II loaded for bear, just about a dozen years later.

To guide our dramatic and quite spectacular chapel liturgies, a certain gifted seminarian (or gifted team) several years ahead of our class had worked out the neatest "how-to" manual I have yet seen. With diagrams reminiscent of those game books kept by basketball and football coaches to direct their players, this mimeographed manual showed exactly where each minister (or "server") was to be, and when. Acolytes, cross bearer, thurifer, lectors, cantors, schola cantorum, subdeacon, deacon, celebrant, master of ceremonies . . .

And then there was that soul-moving Gregorian Chant, sung full throat by about 400 men in cassocks. On high feast days, a first-class polyphonic choir rendered musical compositions worthy of Carnegie Hall. How they made the welkin ring! Envious angels certainly dropped by to listen. Maybe even to sing along.

Those liturgies were some of the most magnificent I have ever seen anywhere, before Vatican II or since. People drove out from Chicago, 20 miles away, in order to watch it all executed with the aplomb and accuracy otherwise expected only of a Benedictine abbey. Which we, of course, were not. But we surely did not live in any liturgical Dark Ages either.

Whatever the word "liturgy" might have meant to seminarians and the religious in those pre-Vatican days, it certainly was not a household word among Catholic laity then, as it is today. Nowadays, anyone remotely connected with weekly school Masses will know how fashionable it is to call those Masses "liturgies," and to involve class after class of grade-school children in the planning of them. Occasionally, those responsible may even need to be reminded that all the essential "planning of liturgy" has already been done at a higher level. It is approved by the Holy See for a given rite, and after that it is not supposed to be tampered with.

Between school Masses and Sunday missalettes, workshops and revved-up liturgy classes, everyone is now familiar with the word "liturgy." Especially as it occurs in "Liturgy of the Word" and "Liturgy of the Eucharist." It is good that the term is so familiar, so well known.

What not everybody knows, or even needs to know, is where the term comes from. As a word in our vocabulary, it is less a translation from the Greek than it is a transliteration. First into Latin, substituting the letters of the Roman alphabet for the Greek ones. Then the new Greco-Latin word was absorbed virtually unchanged into our modern languages, like English, Spanish, Italian, German, French. . . . In the process, enough of its verbal DNA remained to trace its origin back to the Greeks, and that should shed some light on its meaning.

It could be important for people-in-the-pews to realize that our saying "liturgy" today is a fancy way of saying "religious service." The Greek Liddell-Scott Lexicon (referred to above) furnishes examples of how the word was originally used to mean, "public works." Work done by the community for the community. Like building bridges and repairing roads; like our present day city departments for water, sewage, filling potholes and collecting garbage. The kind of services people always need when they live in a community; the kind of things their tax dollars now pay for, things which used to be done by volunteer work or conscription.

Already several centuries before Christ, no less a Greek master than Aristotle extended the term to include service rendered to the gods. Religious service. Then, in Bible talk, the same Greek word was used by the LXX translators in Nm. 8:25 for Levitical service; it is used again in Lk. 1:23 when the future father of John the Baptist does his stint of priestly service in the temple.

Now, however much people may hear a phrase like "Liturgy of the Word." they do not always realize that liturgy means a religious service. And that the "word" in this context refers to the word of God in the Bible. So "Liturgy of the Word" translates to "Bible Service." It is good for Catholics to realize that Protestants by no means have a monopoly on Bible services. Our Church holds them too. Every day in fact. Part One of every Mass we offer is always a genuine Bible service. Even though we choose to call it, in churchspeak, Liturgy of the Word.

All too often, a priest meets fallen-away Catholics. People who (in Texas jargon, probably used elsewhere as well) will tell you that they have "changed religions." In our "new" church, they proudly report, we read the Bible. Well, didn't you ever hear the Bible read in church when you were still a Catholic? Never! Then either you never came to church, or you did not pay attention. Because the Bible is read at every Catholic Mass. (Unfortunately, not all parish sound systems make it easy, or even possible, to understand what is being read. Could the same be said of many lectors?)

In chapter 2, number 51 of the Liturgy Constitution, the Fathers of Vatican II approved comparing this liturgy-of-the-word ("Bible service") to a table where the children of God are fed. The food in question being none other than the Scriptures. Accustomed as we were to calling Holy Communion "the Table of the Lord," some of us at first balked at the way the Council seemed to put preaching and Bible reading on a par with the Eucharist. It sounded so . . . Protestant! The Bible was indeed the word of God in a book; but it could never be equal to the Word of God in Person, the Word Made Flesh, the Word dwelling among us to be our food (Jn. 6).

Once again, the problem was with our thinking. Thinking "either/or" when we should have been thinking "both/and." Indeed, the Scripture can never be on a par with Christ. The word-in-the-Book can never never rival (much less equal) Him Who is The-Word-in-Person, The-Word-Made-Flesh, Word written with a capital "W." Yet both are truly, each in a very real sense, the Word of God. Both are truly in a very real sense our spiritual food. The Liturgy of the Word can truly be one way then, one table, for feeding the family of God spiritually, just as Holy Communion feeds us spiritually in quite another way.

That said, the metaphor of eating at table readily lends itself to further reflection. We have to DIGEST what we INGEST, if it is to do us any good at all. It is not enough to TAKE IN nourishment, we have to TAKE IT APART. Chew on it, break it down, digest it, take it apart so that the parts can be built into our body wherever they are needed or wherever they might be useful. Some parts of the food thus broken down will become skin or bone or muscle. Other parts might turn into nerve tissue or blood, or even (entirely too much) fat. The point is: the food you take in has to become a part of yourself. It cannot and will not do that unless you ruminate on it, digest it, break it down and absorb it.

That is why a homily or sermon is an integral part of the Liturgy of the Word (Const. Lit. nos. 35 and 52). It has been so ever since the days of St Justin the Martyr in the second century (Apology n. 67, read in the breviary on the Third Sunday of Easter). Most likely, it was done even before that. Homilies are supposed to take the scripture reading and break it down, digest it, take it apart so that each hearer can build this or that part into himself or herself, wherever it may be needed. Of course, this is only the beginning. Individual meditation is supposed to continue at home the process which the homily begins in church.

The homily, the breaking down or application part, is where the action of the Lord, the Word using the Voice, becomes important. Often enough (probably more often than anyone realizes), Christ the Lord, the Word speaking with the Voice of the priest or deacon, takes a few words and "zaps" some unsuspecting member of the congregation. The present writer does not want to cite a (very striking) case from his own early preaching days, for fear of violating the secrecy of the confessional. You never know!

What he can do safely is, cite a similar case which he read about "somewhere." A certain priest reported that he suddenly went blank while preaching, completely lost the thread of his prepared discourse. He kept on talking, though, perhaps on the theory that if you run out of ammunition you keep on firing, lest the enemy become aware of your plight.

So this priest kept talking, saying anything at all, until he picked up the lost thread again. Afterwards, a gentleman approached him and said, "Father, when you abandoned your prepared text there for a couple of minutes, you answered in just a few words a major problem that has been bothering me a lot lately." The astonished priest had no idea what he had said during that interval. Me, I can understand that.

In this writer's opinion, bringing out the structure of the Mass as two liturgies was a major achievement of Vatican II. Ungracious and unfair as it is to bad-mouth those pre-Council days, as if everything we did then was wrong, the new Liturgy/Word and Liturgy/Eucharist division is far superior to the "three principal parts of the Mass, offertory, consecration, and communion" that we learned back then. Which, by the way, prompted certain people to stray in late, "but before the priest uncovered the chalice"; and then leave early, right after the priest's communion. Before he even had a chance to say, "Go, the Mass is over," and then get upset if people took him up on it and actually went!

To keep "the two liturgies" balanced and in proper perspective, there is even a different space now assigned to each. Typically, the Liturgy of the Word is held at the microphone-and-lectern, while the Liturgy of the Eucharist takes place at an altar-table.

In most cases, more of a table than an altar. The table aspect is already highlighted by tablecloth and candlelight, ritual dishes and ritual food. Many remodeled modern sanctuaries then carry the meal-and-table theme a step farther, coming up with something that greatly resembles a dining-room table. Thus the "meal" aspect of the Mass is moved ever more forcibly to the foreground, while the "sacrifice" aspect of it (which an altar-like altar would recall) is moved to the rear, and is even more easily lost sight of. Already some catechetical manuals speak only about a meal when they try to explain the Eucharist to young people.

It may be objected that this is precisely what Holy Communion is all about. For the Eucharistic Liturgy IS a Meal: it is The Lord's Supper, as Protestant Christians are wont to call it. "Eat My flesh and drink My blood," said the Lord (Jn. 6:53–58). So what could be wrong with having this meal served from something that so much resembles a dining-room table? Seems very appropriate!

A great many errors are due to focusing on something that is indeed true, but is not the whole story. Being true, it is utterly convincing. One even wonders why other people cannot see something that is so evident. So evidently true! Yes: we moderns do associate eating with a meal, with a table. So did people of the Bible (though the Last Supper table probably did not look exactly like DaVinci envisioned it 15 centuries later).

But for people living in Bible times, eating was ALSO bound up with another occasion that was not one of their regular daily meals. When they offered sacrifice to their God, eating of the victim was an essential part, was THEIR part, in the sacrifice. Only in the case of a real "holocaust" was the victim totally consumed by fire, so that there was no eating involved. We in our generation have overlooked the "totally" part, accustomed as we are to hearing the word holocaust used to characterize a massacre which, however regrettable, still fell short of total destruction. In real Bible talk, holocausts destroyed their victims entirely.

The usual form of animal sacrifices, however, went more like this: the victim was indeed slain, but only as a prelude to being eaten, being consumed in the company of their God (or god). Take the paschal lamb, for instance. Not only an animal sacrifice but a preeminent one, since it formed part of their Great Liberation from Egypt, and it foreshadowed the sacrifice of Him Who was later called the Lamb of God, liberating God's people from servitude to sin and Satan. Eating the Passover was (and is) not just a meal but a religious service; and those who like to reproduce it for teenage CCD classes might well reflect on that fact.

When the paschal lamb was sacrificed, the Chosen People were commanded to eat both its flesh and its internal organs (Ex. 12:8–9). For regular peace offerings, as in Lv. chapter 3, and sin offerings (Lv. ch. 4), the fat and kidneys and liver of the victim were to be burned on the altar by the priest "as food of the Lord's oblation" (Lv. 3:11). These soft interior parts were God's portion in the meal that they were sharing with Him. They themselves were ordered how to eat their part (Lv. 19:5–6). No ordinary meal! Sacrifice was sharing food with God. Unclean animals could not be eaten, so they could not be used as sacrificial victims either (Lv. 27:11).

There is another reference to the sacrificial eating of victims in I Sm. 2:12–17, which recounts the wickedness of the sons of Eli: "When someone offered a sacrifice, the servant of the priest would come while the meat was still boiling, and whatever his fork brought up would be taken away." The servant also demanded raw victim meat, "even before the fat was burned" (v. 15). Evidently, the persons who were offering the sacrifice were used to eating part of the victim, but they were not supposed to forget to leave the Lord His share in the eating of it.

Even among non-Jews in Bible times, the eating of the victim was part of the ceremony: it went with the offering of a sacrifice. This is why the Christians of Corinth brought their case of conscience to Paul (1 Cor. 8:1–13). Could they eat meat that had been sacrificed to idols? Would that not be sharing in the pagan sacrifice?

Paul pointed out that false gods do not really exist, and you can't share a meal with someone who does not even exist. On the other hand, if someone were to see a fellow Christian "reclining at table in the temple of an idol" (v. 10), they might be scandalized. Not just shocked, but literally scandalized. Led to imitate something which they themselves regarded as an act of idolatry, sharing by eating, sharing in a sacrifice offered to a false god.

Whatever is sold at the market, says Paul (1 Cor. 10:25), that you can eat, no questions asked. However, should someone remark that this meat has been offered in sacrifice, then don't eat it (v. 28). Evidently, the common understanding around Corinth saw a link between animal sacrifice and the eating of the victim.

Where are we going with all this? We want to emphasize that, for a scriptural mentality, there is more than one kind of eating. More than just regular daily meals with the family. That was eating indeed, the ordinary dining-room-table kind; but that was not the only kind. There was also the "eating-of-a-sacrifice" kind, the kind associated with an altar and a sacrificial victim. Could our altars honor this, looking like altars as well as dining-room-tables? Could the very furniture of our sanctuary speak of sacrifice as well as a family meal?

It is, or should be, common knowledge that the official teaching of the Church has always been that the Mass is a sacrifice. See, for instance, a Profession of Faith against the Waldenses in 1208 A.D.; the Fourth Lateran Council against the Albigenses and others in 1215 A.D.; the Council of Trent, session xxii in 1562 A.D. against the Reformation. What many Vatican-era writers and educators seem to overlook is that such official condemnations came about because someone was stressing the meal and denying the sacrifice. If this caused a reaction then, because it led the people of God into error, we ought to learn from history. Promoting the same error several centuries later does not make it any less harmful now, nor any less wrong. It may be objected that no one who is now promoting the meal aspect is thereby denying the sacrifice aspect of the Mass. However, leaving it completely out of our teaching is perilously close to denying it altogether.

At very least, it cannot be claimed that the meal idea is something totally new, something that is a theological advance over Trent. Much of what was regarded as "new" in the twentieth century had already been brought up by heretics and schismatics a thousand years ago. Long before Trent or the Reformation.

The bottom line is this: The eating that we do in Holy Communion can and should be regarded as a religious and spiritual meal shared with all the children of God. It brings us together in a common union, a "communion." However, not instead of all this but in addition to it, we must not lose sight of Holy Communion as a sacrificial eating, one that unites us to the victim, to Christ and to God. To represent Communion as merely a meal together, without any reference to the sacrifice or the victim of the cross, is a gross misrepresentation, one that our fathers in the faith reacted against centuries ago. Let's not be so narrow-minded as to focus on only one aspect of the Mass. We have to see it whole to see it right.

*   *   *

If we really want to get close to the Lord Jesus, there is no better way to do it than in the Mass. The Mass, with its twofold liturgy, its twofold table of the children of God. In the Liturgy of the Word, listen for Him Who IS the Word. Don't expect to hear voices to sound in your ears, don't expect private revelations. Just pay careful attention to whatever voice DOES sound in your ears, though. Whatever voice He uses when the Scriptures are read or commented on, within the framework of the Mass, Part One.

The Lord is here. Remember that noble paragraph no. 7 in the Liturgy Constitution, detailing the various ways in which Christ is present in Liturgy. Be aware of His presence when the Scriptures are officially read; in the voice of the preacher commenting on them as well. Be aware, but also beware of a subtle error being smuggled in by some, who fight against calling the Eucharist, the "Real Presence" on the specious grounds that "these other presences are real too."

No one said they weren't: and yet the tradition that gave us the term "Real Presence" is a healthy one, stressing that it is not

ONLY symbolic, but the real flesh and blood of the real Lord. Under cover of theological sophistication, of being hip to a new kind of theological thinking, some people are trying to downplay the importance of the Eucharist: as if refusing to call it the "Real Presence" were evidence of a clearer, more updated understanding.

Unfortunately, experience shows that someone will always fall for this fallacy, and it's too bad. Especially when it is allegedly done in the name of the Lord. However, the devil's ploy can alert us to the importance of what is under Enemy attack.

Of course, calling the Eucharist or Blessed Sacrament "the Real Presence" is in no way meant to imply that the other ways of being present are NOT real. It merely insists, and rightly so, that this one IS real. Pope Paul VI already explained that in his 1965 encyclical "Mysterium Fidei," pointing out how the Eucharistic presence of Christ is truly special. Here, the God-Man in Person is present in the fullest sense, whole and entire. And just in case anyone missed that explanation, it was repeated almost forty years later, in 2003, by Pope John Paul II in "Ecclesia de Eucharistia." No amount of New Theology, which contradicts this papal teaching, should keep us from finding the Lord Christ "really there" in Holy Communion.

And when we do find Him, the best possible use of this close encounter with the Lord might well be the prayer of silence. A prayer that says nothing at all, a prayer thinking no thoughts at all, a prayer that is simply and solely aware of His nearness, a prayer eager to absorb as much as possible of His awesome love. Just hold still, like a child in its mother's lap, and let the Good Lord love you a little. Don't interrupt.

Try to be as empty as possible (following St Augustine's advice) so that He may fill you with more of His love and grace. Don't even try transmitting any messages to Him right now: you can do that later. Just now, while He is downloading what HE wants to see in our souls, we don't want to interrupt. We hold ourselves in a receiving mode rather than a sending one. Open and submit to the Incoming Word, Who is perfectly capable of saving our souls (Jas. 1:21). Without help or interference.

Thus, the Liturgy of the Mass becomes a two-way street as well as a twofold table. By it, we go to God; more important, by it, God comes to us. Could anything be more awesome?

Part Two

Selected Homilies for Feasts

Preaching the Voice and the Word

Preliminary Remarks

Preaching is a very personal thing. Anyone who has read this far will be aware of our conviction that it is actually a two-person enterprise. Christ the Lord as the main person, plus some deacon or priest as His spokesperson, a voice on loan to the Word.

The "Voice and the Word" fits the biblical model of prophets. Prophets were not necessarily people who could foresee and foretell future events, though they sometimes did that, too. Their main function, however, the role that really made a man a prophet, was this: To enunciate in audible human acoustic tones, in personal speech, a message that came from a supra-human and supra-acoustic, but definitely very personal God.

So preaching, like "propheting," is a very personal task, a person speaking a message from a Person. Reading aloud from someone else's script, even reading one's own pre-typed message, is too impersonal a way to go about it.

God is the Transcendent One, out of our league and beyond our human experience. At our human level He communicates by means of human voices speaking. Any attempt to insert a third party in between the Word and the Voice is a risky venture, perhaps one doomed to failure. The "voice" (preacher, whether priest or deacon) may indeed be helped by a homiletic service, either one purchased alone or as part of a magazine subscription. But only on condition that the material so offered is thoroughly digested by the homilist prior to his homily. Let it become so much a part of him that it can be truly SPOKEN from the heart, not simply read off a typed or printed page. As a source of homiletic material, nothing can ever substitute for the Word within. Nothing: not even *le dernier cri,* the newest in theological-biblical research.

Sometimes the homilist may find that the proffered material is indigestible. Excellent scholarship, perhaps: but his spiritual digestive tract rejects it rather than absorbs it. Individual bits of information may be gratefully incorporated into his own outline, but the homily itself definitely has to be his own.

This is said as a disclaimer to the homily-meditations that follow. It is not our intention that anyone should be able to use them for preaching just as they stand. However, should anyone find that he can use an idea here or there, he is welcome to take it. To adapt or adopt, as he may see fit.

This little book, if it sees the light of day, might also prove helpful to a certain number of non-preachers, people who simply want to meditate on the Gospel for a given feast or Sunday. If the Good Lord in His capacity as The Word wishes to speak by these written words here, if He chooses to "reach out and touch someone" through these written lines as He seems to have done when they were spoken in church . . . Well, that would make the writer very happy.

"Every scribe who has learned about the kingdom can be compared to the head of a household, who brings forth from his storeroom both new things and old" (Mt 13:52). Behold, then, a mixed menu, a salad containing both "new things and old." God grant that no one may feel like quoting a review from an old movie: "parts that are new and parts that are good; the good parts are not new and the new parts are not good." If that be so, we apologize in advance!

Advent—First Sunday

I

Today is the first Sunday of Advent. Exactly what does the word "Advent" mean to you? I am sure that you have been told every year that "advent" means the arrival or the coming of something. Webster's unabridged dictionary gives this as an example: "the advent of atomic power in industry."

So it's possible to use the word in ordinary speech, a non-religious context, even if we don't do that very often. In religious speech, talking liturgically, we are really quite used to the word already. Every Catholic knows that Advent is a time when we get prepared spiritually for Christmas. We are getting ready to celebrate the Lord's "coming to earth" as a Baby at Bethlehem.

For centuries, that WAS the focus of the four Sundays of Advent: namely, Christ's coming to the world at Christmas. About forty years ago, a new dimension was added. The idea or ideal of a spiritual Christmas preparation is still there, but it's only from December 17th to December 24th.

Before that, from the first Sunday of Advent till December 16th, the liturgy does try to prepare us spiritually for the coming of the Lord. Only, it focuses on His SECOND Coming. Coming back at the end of the world, coming back to judge the living and dead.

II

History testifies that people in every century have always been interested in the Second Coming of Christ. Very interested. Eager to hear all possible inside information. Especially: WHEN is it going to happen? Soon? Will it be in my lifetime?

People who ask such questions do have some faith: they believe the Second Coming is going to happen. Unfortunately, popular interest is focused largely on WHEN it is going to happen, and that is the one thing God isn't telling us. The Lord Jesus Himself said that even the angels of God did not know that (Mt. 24:36, Mk. 13:32). In fact, He said He did not know that either. So if anyone tells you they now have some new information on the timing (like Seventh Day Adventists and those who talk about the Rapture). . . . Just don't listen to them.

Instead of asking WHEN (which we cannot possibly know), let's focus on something else about the Second Coming that we CAN know. Something that might make us feel a bit more comfortable about that Great Day of Wrath, the Day of Judgment. Namely, that it IS about "judgment." And if you understand judgment in the biblical sense, that can be good news indeed. Christ is coming as our Judge in the biblical sense. What does that mean?

In the Bible, in the Old Testament Book of Judges, the "judges" were heaven-sent saviors of their people. Judges were men like Gideon, Jephthah, or Samson, whom God raised up to be leaders of His people when they needed one. When they needed a leader to save them from death and destruction.

Now we all know that Jesus is the Savior of God's People. Before He was even born, the angel gave this divine order to St. Joseph: Mary's Son was to be called by the name of "Jesus," a name that in Hebrew means "God Saves," or "Divine Savior." "Call Him Jesus," said the angel, "because He will save His people" (Mt. 1:21).

So Jesus Christ is our Savior. In the early pages of the Bible, the savior of the people was a "judge." This "Judge" too Who is Jesus comes to *save.* This is not just my idea. At the beginning of Mass, one of the short "penitential" prayers is built around the "Coming of the Lord." A coming past, present, and future. Past, "You CAME to gather the nations." Present, "You COME in *word* and *sacrament.*" Future, "You WILL COME in glory WITH SALVATION for God's People. . . ." Notice: you will come with SALVATION.

In the First Preface for Advent, the Church herself prays: "Now we watch for the day, hoping that the SALVATION PROMISED US WILL BE OURS WHEN CHRIST THE LORD WILL COME AGAIN IN HIS GLORY."

III

Our whole point in today's homily is this: The Second Coming of Christ at the end of the world is something for us to look forward to, expecting it eagerly instead of fearing and dreading it. Almost the last line of the Bible ends with the wish: "Come, Lord Jesus!" Early Christian communities kept this Aramaic expression in their liturgy: "Marana tha!" (1 Cor. 16:22). A word from the language of the Lord, like "Amen" and "Alleluja." Marana tha: Come, Lord!

Oh, sure! You can read chapter 25 of St. Matthew's Gospel about the last judgment, separating sheep from goats, sending the goats into hell-fire. "Depart from Me, ye cursed, into everlasting fire. . . ."

But He also says to those on His right: "Come, ye blessed of My Father; take possession of the kingdom that has been prepared for you" (Mt. 25:34). After all, you have tried to be faithful, or you wouldn't be here in church today. If we were perfect, we wouldn't need a Savior. Since we realize we need one, let's just be glad that we have One. Let's trust Him to do His job.

Trust Jesus to be "Jesus," to be "a God Who saves." Trust Him to accomplish the task His Heavenly Father gave Him. Looking at the world around us, it does not seem saved, it is definitely not free from sin and wrong. Don't be impatient! The saving process has been started; it just isn't finished yet.

Around this time of the year, some of you may have purchased Christmas gifts and had them put on layaway. As I understand it, those items are already set aside for you in the store; they just haven't been delivered to you yet because the final payment is still outstanding. Well, salvation for us and for our world is already a sure thing. It will be ours when Christ our Lord will come to make the final payment. He will do that at His Second Coming. Now why should THAT be something for us to be afraid of?

Christmas from Luke 2

I

Most of you are probably familiar with computers and search engines. Search engines like "Google," where you can type in a single word, and the computer calls up a flood of titles from its collective memory, and displays them on a screen in front of you.

Our minds work something like that. Say "Christmas," and see what a flood of imagery wells up. All the thoughts and memories that you have learned to associate with Christmas. Children might have visions of Santa Claus, of toys and presents and even of Rudolph the Red-Nosed Reindeer. For adults, there may be special thoughts of some Christmas past: Christmas trees and decorations; food and family and church; the music of "Silent Night" and "Jingle Bells"; visions of the Christ Child, of Christmas cribs and manger scenes, of glory to God and peace on earth.

Before you were very old, you would have seen many pictures of the Bethlehem scene. Christmas cards, and many of the traditional Nativity sets that we call Christmas cribs. And you never tire of hearing again the age-old story of the birth of Christ, no matter how often you have read it or heard it already.

The favorite version of that Christmas story, the one that has influenced countless poets and preachers, artists and Christian people down through the centuries, that favorite version is what we read in the second chapter of St. Luke's Gospel. Everybody else got the story from Luke. Where did Luke get it? What was the source of his information?

II

It's all there. All in Luke's Gospel. Shepherds and angels, Mary and Joseph, the Infant wrapped in swaddling clothes and lying in a manger, because there was no room for them at the inn. This is the Bible account. The real story. The Gospel story. This is Luke.

We are all familiar with what he wrote. But where did he get it? A lot of devout Christians would instinctively answer, from God. After all, this is the Bible. This is a divinely-inspired account, so it must be from God. God not only inspired Luke to write it up, God must have told Luke what he should write. Makes sense, no?

Well, that is not what Luke himself says. It is not what the Bible itself says about where Luke got his material. Right in the opening verses of his Gospel, Luke tells all the world that before sitting down to write his Gospel, he checked with eyewitnesses (Lk. 1:2).

Then he proceeds to tell us about Nazareth and Bethlehem, about the angel bringing a message from God to a girl of Nazareth named Mary; a message about her conceiving a baby who would be the very Son of the Most High, the very Son of God. Luke tells us how that baby came to be born in Bethlehem, the city of David, instead of in Mary's own hometown of Nazareth. In short, Luke's first two chapters read like memories told by a certain eyewitness named Mary. Mary, who twice in this Lucan narrative (Lk. 2:19 and 2:51) is said to have kept all these things in her heart, going over them again and again during all the years that followed. Kept turning them over in her own mind, until one day Luke showed up to ask her, what do YOU remember about Him?

Now don't be surprised if some priest tells you about modern Bible scholars, even very good scholars, who have other ideas about the origin of these so-called infancy narratives. You can follow them if you want. You won't be expelled from the Church.

74

Just be aware that by doing so, you are setting aside the plain testimony of the Bible itself. Even contradicting Luke's own claim to his sources, his claim about where he got his information.

"Tracing the whole sequence of events from the beginning," as he put it (Lk. 1:1–2), Luke was led to Mary, who was personally there at the very beginning. Mary, the only possible eyewitness to all five "joyful mysteries of the rosary." Mary, whom the Bible explicitly says kept all such memories in her heart. Kept them in reserve for Luke, and thereby preserved the facts for all of us.

On this Christmas feast, you have listened to the human voice of a deacon or a priest, reading aloud once again the timeless story of the first Christmas. Behind that voice is the God-inspired printed page of the Gospel. Behind that printed page, behind that Gospel, is the Evangelist Luke who first wrote it down. Wrote down the memories of Mary, the Mother of Jesus—Mary, who was there!

You might have heard this already. Or, reflecting on the Gospel text, you might have figured it out for yourself. Or maybe you are hearing this for the first time, Some people will tell you it isn't so; however, just read what Luke says about eyewitnesses and then ask yourself who else could have witnessed what he is telling us. Then you might want to thank Mary, the Mother of Jesus, not only for having given us the Christ Child, but for having given us the beautiful story of Christmas. A story that she kept alive in her heart, so that it could be shared with you and with me, and with all the world until the end of time.

Epiphany

Today's Feast of the Epiphany is very old. So old that it goes back to the earliest times of our Christian Catholic religion. It is based, of course, on the second chapter of St. Matthew's Gospel, which tells the story just as you heard it read to you today.

Every generation of Christians has heard the same story. The story itself, however, has taken on different meanings for different ages, different times, different cultures. It should not surprise us if we find some new message, some new emphasis, for people today, in this our twenty-first century.

At the beginning, the Christian Church faced a problem that we no longer worry about, at least not in the same exact form as then. You can learn more about that problem of Early Christians by a careful reading of the Acts of the Apostles and the Epistles of St. Paul. You just have to know what you are looking for, or you might not even notice it when you read the Bible today.

The problem was caused in those early days by having two kinds of converts to the infant Church. Some had grown up as Jews, while others had not. For reasons that we can readily understand, those coming in from a Jewish background brought a lot of their own baggage with them. Lots of Jewish beliefs and practices that they had grown up with. Some older Catholics should be able to understand that, Catholics who were faced with changes they did not like in the Church after the Second Vatican Council. Like Jewish converts in the first couple of centuries, they protested that "this is what I was brought up on."

Converted Christians who had been "Cradle Jews" brought

with them into the Church a lot of ideas like the need for circumcision, the Law of Moses, religious customs and feasts and taboos that seemed perfectly natural and sensible to them. They could even trace such things back to the Bible. Hadn't God revealed the Old Testament as a prelude to the New? How was it possible to enter the Church without first passing through the vestibule? Many of these Jewish converts felt that people converting from a pagan background would first have to become Jews in order to become Christians at all.

We now know that they were wrong. St. Paul and his friends knew it too, and fought those tendencies tooth and nail. They rightly took the position, approved by the Apostles at a special meeting in Jerusalem, that the New Testament was indeed New. Perhaps St. Matthew as well, in writing chapter two of his Gospel, wanted to convey the same message: Namely, God was revealing His Son Jesus to be the Savior of all mankind: not just the Jews, but the Gentiles also. The Savior, Matthew is saying here, is being revealed to non-Jews, represented by these Magi for whom God sent a special guiding star that would lead them to Jesus.

II

Centuries passed. This message about salvation for non-Jews was eventually taken for granted, but it took quite a while. In Rome, there is a big fifth-century mosaic in Santa Sabina Church on the Aventine Hill; it shows two equal and identical women, one of them labeled "Church from the Synagogue" and the other labeled, "Church from the Gentiles." As late as the early 400s, that still had to be emphasized. Co-existing, both equal, both belonging to the same Church.

Of course, in every century, Christians continued to reflect on the Gospel pages, including this page with the story of the Magi. New thoughts kept cropping up, new conclusions were drawn.

That there must have been three Magi, for instance, because there were three gifts: gold, frankincense, and myrrh. And the Magi must have been kings, they reasoned. Because the Book of Psalms has a prophecy (Ps. 72:10–11) about kings from far-off lands bringing their gifts and paying homage to God's Anointed One. After all, doesn't the very word "Christ" mean "the Anointed One"?

Then, in medieval times, Christmas cribs became common. And there in full view, Christian people saw tiny statues of three kings, complete with their gifts and their camels. Names were invented for "The Three Kings": Gaspar, Melchior, and Balthasar. They quickly represented the three continents of the then-known world: Europe, Asia, and Africa. The African one was duly given a black face. Testimony to a healthy feeling that Christianity was indeed meant to be Catholic, meant to be universal. There was room at Bethlehem for all races, for all the world.

Attention focused not only on the Magi but also on their gifts. Gold for the great King Jesus; incense offered to the truly divine Son of God; myrrh for His human body that would some day be buried with this chemical substance (Jn. 19:39). Some saw in the three gifts the symbols of our own offering to the Christ Child: the gold of love, the incense of prayer, the bitter myrrh that stood for mortification, suffering, and death to self.

In Northern European countries, the reputed initials of the three Wise Men were chalked on the doorposts and lintels of people's houses on the Feast of Epiphany, to ask their protection and their prayers for the new year just beginning.

In Spain and Italy, this became the day for people to give gifts to their children, because the Magi brought gifts to the Christ Child. Spanish youngsters sometimes put out hay for the camels of "los Reyes"—something like American youngsters putting out cookies and milk for Santa Claus. In Italy, the word Epiphany has been metamorphosed into the name "Befana." Befana is a roving witch who at this time brings toys or lumps of coal to Italian children, depending on whether the recipient had been good or bad.

III

These are nice customs, part of some interesting folklore. Can we draw some new conclusions in the light of our twenty-first century world? What thoughts will arise in our hearts as we contemplate these turban-wearing figures from the Middle East? From Arabia or Iraq or Afghanistan? All following the crescent moon of Islam rather than the star of Bethlehem?

If you read different commentators or even different translations of the Bible, you may notice a little disagreement about whether we ought to read, "We in the East have seen His star" or: "We have seen His star in the East." What's in the East: the star or the people who are looking at it? Actually, the Gospel text itself reads, "Magi FROM THE EAST arrived in Jerusalem" (Mt. 2:1). So the people, the original Magi, were from regions East of Jerusalem, East of the Jordan River. Which covers a lot of territory, all of it Muslim territory today!

Today, then, the lineal descendants of the Magi put Mohammed ahead of Christ. That ought to worry us, or at least, it ought to make us feel bad. How about a silent prayer to the Magi today, to those Wise Men of old, so that through their intercession these descendants of theirs may share in the Wise Men's wisdom, the wisdom of God? And follow it like a star that will lead them, at long last, to the feet of Christ. After all, He came for them, too.

Baptism of Christ

Today we celebrate the Feast of the Baptism of Christ. The Church wants us to reflect upon His baptism, and our own.

I

For many centuries, the remembrance of the Lord's baptism was tucked away inside the Feast of the Epiphany. The very word "epiphany" means a revelation, a manifestation, a "showing forth," or a public appearance. The one feast of the Epiphany groups together three major times when Christ the Lord was revealed, was "shown forth," was officially presented to the world.

When Jesus was born, God the Father wanted to show His Son to the world, much as proud parents (who, after all, are made in His image, so there is a resemblance between the Father and human parents . . .). Proud parents, we're saying, like to show off THEIR children. Especially if it's a new baby. Baby's arrival on the world scene is announced to all and sundry, announced to all the members of the extended family, so that everybody can come trooping by, eager to see and admire the new baby in the family.

Think of God the Father doing something like that. Judean shepherds, representing the Chosen People, got a special angelic birth announcement, and they walked across the fields of Bethlehem to have a look. The non-Jewish Magi living in Eastern lands were invited by an special star, and they followed it to find and worship the newborn King. Such was the first presentation of

Christ to the world, a presentation, an epiphany, at the time of His birth.

A second time, when Christ is already grown up and is about to begin His career, His "public life," God the Father reveals Him again. Once again, God the Father presents His Son to the world at the Jordan River, where John was baptizing. When Jesus steps up to be baptized, God the Father says publicly, "This is My Son. I'm proud of Him!!" Well-pleased with Him, proud of Him. (Traditionally, the Church also celebrated a third epiphany, a third manifestation of Jesus on this feast day. There was another official revelation, another public appearance when Jesus worked His first miracle, changing water into wine at a wedding feast in Cana of Galilee. The story is told in John's Gospel, and John concludes the account by saying [Jn. 2:11] that in this way, Jesus "revealed His glory" so that His disciples would believe in Him, would take Him seriously. Revealed His glory, His divinity, "epiphanized it." Since John used that word, the official liturgy of the day included the Miracle of Cana as being a kind of epiphany too.)

We celebrated the coming of the Magi last Sunday. Today, we are concentrating on the Baptismal "epiphany." An occasion when God the Heavenly Father announces publicly that He is pleased with the way His Son has turned out. You can understand human parents feeling that way, and talking that way, about their grown children who have turned out well. Why not God? Since Adam and Eve, the first human parents, were made in the image and likeness of God (Gn. 1:26–27), we should not balk at finding a resemblance between parents and God. It's a two-way street. Parents are like God in many ways, and God is like human parents.

Think how eager human parents are to show off their new baby. Think how proud they are when their son-or-daughter grows up enough to hit their first home run. When they graduate from college with high honors. When they are launched on what will surely be a brilliant career. Now you can imagine how God the Father felt about His Son, and He too had to tell the whole world.

"I am well pleased," He says in all three synoptic Gospels (Mt. 3 verse 17; Mk. 1:11; Lk. 3:22). We can draw a conclusion here, we can apply this to our own lives in some small way. Let's strive hard to make God pleased with us too. We can't turn water into wine, like Jesus did at Cana of Galilee. But in some small way, in the place where God has put us and with the talents He has given us, we can try to do well the work that He has assigned to us personally. Do it so well that God is going to be pleased with us too. Well pleased. Make your Heavenly Father proud of you, the way He was proud of Jesus. Well-pleased.

II

By making a special feast for the Baptism of Christ separate from the other two epiphanies, the Church evidently wants us to think about our own baptism as well. She will remind us about it again at Easter, when we are asked to renew our baptismal promises and we get sprinkled with water as a reminder. At the Easter Vigil and Easter Masses, there is a kind of communal celebration of our own baptismal anniversary.

However, at Easter time, our focus will be on the Resurrection of the Lord, so the anniversary of our own baptism will take a back seat. Let's take a few minutes right now to move mentally from the Baptism of the Lord to our own baptism.

Of course, it is not exactly the same thing. The ceremony that was presided over by John the Baptist that day at the Jordan River, was not a sacrament instituted by Christ, like our baptisms today.

Our baptism makes us children of God (which is a more positive way of saying we are freed from original sin, which is the LACK of God in us). Christ did not need any ceremony to make Him the Son of God: He was already Son of God by nature. "Begotten" as such—Son of God not even "by birth," but by "generation"!!

Nonetheless, there is a resemblance between His baptism and our own. Both of them, in different ways, officially dissociated us from sin and Satan. Our lives, like His, were officially consecrated to God. Today is a good time for us to renew that intention, that resolve, that official dedication to God and to His plan for our salvation, a plan to which Christ was dedicating His life there and then. At our own baptism, a tiny River Jordan flowed across our forehead; we were born again of water and the Spirit (Jn. 3:5); we were all assigned a place, our own place, in the Kingdom of God.

Let's be proud of our citizenship in that kingdom, much like many of our fellow citizens who display a bumper sticker that says they are "proud to be an American." Be proud to be a citizen of God's Kingdom and make God your Father proud of you too!

The Tempting of Christ

Gospel for First Sunday of Lent, Years A, C
(Lect. Nos. 22 & 24)

Each year on the First Sunday of Lent, the Church shows us Christ the Lord fasting and tempted in the desert. Then also each year, on the Second Sunday of Lent, we contemplate Christ the Lord in His glory, transfigured on a mountaintop.

The Transfiguration bears witness to the Lord's real divinity. The very voice of God the Father tells us that He is truly the Son of God. On the other hand, His desert experience, which you heard about today, bears witness to His real humanity. That He is just as truly a Son of Man as He is Son of God. Man enough, human enough, to get hungry when He fasts, just like we do. He is also human enough to be tempted by the devil, even as we are.

As believing Christians, we have no problem with accepting His divinity. So in a way, nothing that He does with superhuman power, like His miracles and His Resurrection, none of that really surprises us. After all, it is just what a person would expect from Him: what you'd expect from the Son of God come into our world.

Where we do have a problem, albeit unconsciously, is in accepting the fact that the Son of Man could be so . . . So HUMAN. We do not expect Him to be tempted, much less tempted by the devil: the way human beings have been tempted by the devil, ever since Eve.

So we listen dutifully to Gospel accounts of Christ's temptations, thinking all the while in the back of our minds that it was really no contest at all. A sort of mock battle where the devil never really had a chance. How could Jesus be tempted? How could He really feel like doing something bad, He Who (for all his human nature) is holiness personified?

There IS a mystery here. Mystery (as in "murder mystery") means that something has really happened (like a murder), but we have no idea who did it, nor how it was done. The EXISTENCE of the fact, we do not doubt. It is the EXPLANATION that eludes us.

In contemplating the temptations of Christ in the desert, we cannot explain how someone human could be truly tempted if He is at the same time divine. It comes down to this: we are at a loss to explain how one and the same person can be truly God and truly man, both at the same time. As man He could be tempted, of course. But He's also God. . . . We can't understand. It's a good thing we don't HAVE TO understand. We just have to BELIEVE. So, we make an act of faith. Which is the right thing to do. Then, to satisfy our own uneasiness, we sort of marginalize the part about a real temptation, and decide not to think about that at all. Which is the wrong thing to do. The reality of the temptation has to be included in our act of faith if we are to believe in the real Christ. Son of God, but also Son of Man.

II

What are some of the conclusions we can draw? We mentioned one of them already: Make an act of faith in the real humanity of Jesus Christ, Son of God. That done, we might move on now to draw three further practical conclusions.

One is from the Epistle to the Hebrews (4:15) in the New Testament. It reads like this: "We do not have the kind of high priest who would be unable to sympathize with our weakness: our High Priest has been tempted/tested like us in every way, though without committing any sin." And again in the next chapter (5:2): "He is able to sympathize and to be patient with the ignorant and the erring since He Himself was beset by weakness."

Secondly—and this seems to be why the liturgy reminds us of His desert fasting at the beginning of Lent—the forty-day fast of Christ in the desert has traditionally been cited as a precedent for our own Lenten fasting. The new edition of the breviary (2000 A.D.) still makes this point three times in Latin Lenten hymns: twice it describes our abstinence as being "quadragenaria" ("fortyish"); for a third time, it still uses a rather lame Latin rhyme "deno dierum circulo, ducto quater notissimo"! (Forty was a time-honored tradition. Leaving out Sundays, you had six full weeks of fast days, 6×6 days = 36. To make up the extra four and to attain a full forty, you added four days. Ash Wednesday to the following Saturday. Thirty-six plus four equals forty. Forty = "Quadragesima," the common name for the Lenten Season. Nevertheless, prior to Vatican II, the Sundays which we left out were still known as "First Sunday of Lent" etc. Moreover, the three preceding Sundays bore the proud names of "Septuagesima, Sexagesima, Quinquagesima . . ." pure Latin for 70th, 60th, 50th! Which they clearly were not, by any form of reckoning. To make matters worse, some monks and hermits in bygone centuries even began their Lenten observance right after the Feast of the Holy Cross, in mid September! So how long IS Lent? The latest Latin Missale Romanum, editio typica 2002 A.D., now flatly states that "Lent runs from Ash Wednesday up to the Mass of Holy Thursday, exclusive." This is n. 28 of the "Normae Universales de Anno Liturgico et Calendarium Romanum Generale"—*not n. 28 of the well-known GIRM, which is a separate section entitled, "Institutio Generalis Missalis Romani."* Any way to get forty days from Ash Wednesday to Holy Thursday, with or without Sundays?)

Glancing back over our history, it seems we have not only failed to follow Christ's example in the forty days, but also failed in the fasting. There are only two real fast days left, apart from recommendations. Expert thinking around the time of Vatican II was extremely considerate of how "modern man" might react to things. In view of modern Americans' preoccupation with dieting, it would seem that we could reintroduce fasting if we only changed the name of it a little!

Thirdly, Fundamentalist Christians like to harass us poor hapless Catholics by quoting the Bible. "The Bible says . . . The Bible says . . . The Bible says." It is interesting to note from this Lenten Sunday Gospel of the Tempting of Christ that even the devil knew how to quote "the Bible" for his own ends. The lesson is obvious. Not everyone who quotes "the word of God" is by that very fact speaking for his God. The devil wasn't then. He isn't now.

Not everyone who quotes the Bible, gets it right. You just have to be careful. Practically every heresy in the history of the Church claimed to be based on the Bible. Most of the time, what they were quoted was actually there—the person quoting it had simply failed to look on the other page. There is no error so convincing as one that contains PART of the truth.

The main point for us to take along is rather, the comforting assurance of Scripture (Hebrews plus the Gospel of the Tempting) that the Lord will understand how we just happened to fall into temptation. After all, He has been there. Though of course in His case, without sin.

The Vine and the Branches
Gospel for the Fifth Sunday of Easter, Year B
(Lect. no. 53)

Five full chapters of St. John's Gospel (13 to 17 inclusive) are de-
voted to what Jesus said to His Apostles on the night of Holy
Thursday. Which is quite a bit, when you consider that the entire
Gospel of John is only 21 chapters long.

I

Right in the midst of the Holy Thursday discourses, we stum-
ble across an unexpected glitch. The little company is all gathered
in the "large upper room" (Mk. 14:15) where they have eaten the
Last Supper, and Jesus has washed the feet of the Apostles. All the
while He has been talking about various topics: two whole chapters' worth, totaling some 70 verses in our modern reckoning.
("Modern," because Scripture was not divided into chapters and
verses until around the time printing was invented.)

At a certain point (Jn. 14:31), Jesus says, "Arise, let us go."
Then in the very next verse, He launches into an extended discourse about Himself as the Vine and His followers as branches.
Which is a very beautiful and thought-provoking comparison, one
that sheds a lot of light on our relationship. Personally, this writer
loves it! However, he couldn't help thinking at first, the Lord Himself just broke up the Last Supper by suggesting that they all leave.

Let's go, he says. Then He goes right on talking. ("Lord—didn't You just say we were leaving?")

II

A minor problem, surely. Well, even minor problems deserve a solution, so here's a suggestion: They do leave. And from the upper room, they go down an outside stairway providing access to the second storey. (On your next pilgrimage to Jerusalem, do not look for either the stairway *or* the room. No matter what your tour guide says, the present building dates from Crusader days, at very earliest. Note the Gothic arches, the groin-vaulted ceiling. . . .)

Outdoor stairway. Grapevines growing on the side of the house, like they do in that part of the world—compare Psalm 127 (128) verse 3: "a vine *on the walls*" (Vulgate not NAB)—maybe even a vine on a trellis over the stairs. Being Passover, it is springtime. In the springtime, the Mediterranean custom is to trim grapevines to within an inch of their life.

So on the way out, the Lord and his Apostles can't help noticing the trimmed vines and the trimmed-off branches on the ground, as they make their way from the upper room to the Kedron Valley and to Gethsemani Orchard on the other side. As always, anything He sees can remind Jesus of the Kingdom. And as He did with His parables, so now too He seizes the opportunity to teach a lesson. Once again, we are grateful to John for having made it possible for us to listen in.

We followers of Christ, we disciples, live by His life in us. We share in what makes Him the Son of God, makes God our Father. Like branchlets on the grapevine, we will stay alive and will bear fruit of holiness and virtue only by remaining attached to Him in faith and love. Firmly attached to, clinging to, Him Who is like the main stalk. Anything separated from Him is like those cut-off vine-branches (gesturing). Branches destined for burning because they are good for nothing else whatever (see and read Ez. 15:1–6).

III

That lesson would have made a deep impression on the Apostles (like John), who were viewing the newly-trimmed vines and the raked-together trimmings by the light of the Passover full moon. It certainly impressed John, because it even impresses us (including many modern Christians from non-grape country, who may never have seen a grapevine in their life). It's either Him, or the fire. To express it more positively, in Him we live and move and have our being (Acts 17:28). This is really what being a Christian is all about. Christ sharing His Life with us. "To those who accepted Him, to them He (The Word Incarnate) gave the power to become children of God" (Jn. 1:12). God becomes the Father of Christians, as God is the Father of the Christ.

Christians are "The Family," not mafia-style, but better: sons and daughters of God, because we share by sanctifying grace in what makes Christ the Son of God. "From His fullness—look up Col. 2:9–10—we have received one grace piled on top of another" (Jn. 1:16; Cat. Catholic Church, N. 1999). As the Mass prayer says at the mixing of water and wine: "We share in His divinity, as He shares in our humanity." What a trade-off!

IV

Just as the main stock or stem of a grapevine pumps its own special life into all the branches and tendrils that sprout from it, so we Christians live by the Life of Christ in us (Gal. 2:20). Not only does this vine-and-branches comparison help us understand our relationship to Christ, it also helps us to understand Church—the

90

relationship which Christians have to one another. To phrase it a different way, the vine-and-branches is one "model" of Church. As an eminent modern theologian has pointed out so well, the biblical understanding of "Church" is expressed in different ways: Mystical Body, People of God, the Flock of the Good Shepherd, a building or a whole city . . . or a Vine and Branches.

Unfortunately, we seem to get stuck with only one metaphor at a time. In the Days of Vatican II, we incessantly heard nothing but People of God, People of God, People of God . . . Prior to that, around mid-century, it was nothing but the Mystical Body. What about the City of God, and God's Temple? Both biblical images, though neither enjoyed much popularity, ever. It would seem that the idea of being a stone, even a living stone, does not have such a broad appeal. Belonging to the "Flock," on the contrary, always did prove attractive, particularly to people who have never had any personal contact with sheep. Still, it is one of the Lord's own metaphors; and maybe being a living animal (however stupid and smelly) is indeed preferable to being a rock in the church wall, or a stone pillar holding up the temple roof.

All the models of Church are merely images, metaphors. All in the tradition of Christ the Lord, Who taught in comparisons and Who saw the Kingdom of God reflected everywhere. However, we may be permitted to have our favorites, and the vine-branches is our own front-runner. Because it says so much, so well, about our relationship with Christ and with one another.

Not to mention the necessity of remaining tightly bonded with Him by love and faith. No sheep shares so much with any shepherd. Nor does the sheep's relationship with its shepherd illustrate as well as the vine-and-branches metaphor the horrible consequences of cutting oneself off from Christ AND the Church. For those who think they can cut themselves off from the Church (the vine) and still remain attached to the main stem, it doesn't work.

Easter
Acts Reading, Years A, B, C (Lect. No. 42)

I

About the same time that we Christians are celebrating our Easter, Jewish People are celebrating their Passover. ("Pesach" they call it.) According to a reliable Jewish source, the annual Pesach celebration is held so that Jews will never forget what God did for their People. Liberated them from Pharaoh and from Egypt.

From your own knowledge of the Old Testament, you are certainly familiar with the general outlines of their story. How they were to sacrifice and consume the paschal lamb, after smearing its blood on the doorposts of their houses so that the Destroying Angel would "pass over" their families without slaying their first-born.

How they had to leave the country by night and in a great hurry. So great a hurry that there was no time to let their bread dough rise. They had to take the unbaked bread dough with them into the desert, and prepare their bread unleavened in the ashes of their campfires (Ex. 12:39).

And finally, how they passed through the waters of the Red Sea and began their long desert trek to the Promised Land.

II

God did all this for His people, and Jewish religious leaders are saying we don't want them to forget it, ever. Christians likewise read it all in the Bible, and believe that God did indeed work these wonders for those who were then His chosen people. For two thousand years, Christians also believed that THEY were now the new chosen people; except for a sophisticated few, most of us believe it yet.

This belief of ours is based on holy Scripture, on the Bible. In union with Peter and Paul and all the followers of the Christian faith since day one, we see the paschal lamb as a prophecy of spiritual salvation from the servitude of sin and Satan. A prophecy that was fulfilled in Christ ("The Lamb of God") and in His sacrificial death on the cross. We believe that we and potentially all peoples of the earth were saved by the Blood of the Lamb. That Christ in a much fuller sense than Moses leads us out of slavery, through the waters of baptism, out across the desert of this life, to a promised land in heaven.

All of which was confirmed by Christ's rising from the dead, just as He foretold. Was His "rising from the dead"—the resurrection we recall at Easter—was it really so important? Yes. Because at least twice, Jesus appealed to it as an official proof that He was really Who He said He was. Let's look at those two times.

(1)

At the cleansing of the temple, when temple officials demanded a sign from Jesus that He was authorized to thus take charge, His cryptic answer was, "Destroy this temple, and in three days (on the third day) I will raise it up again." His enemies took that to mean the temple building, the construction of which had taken forty-six years. At Jesus' trial, they would twist His words into a threat, a threat to destroy Jerusalem's most sacred shrine (Mk. 14:58).

According to John, the Apostles themselves were no less

puzzled. Only later, in the light of Easter and Christ's unexpected resurrection, only then were they able to understand that "He was talking about the temple of His own Body" (Jn. 2:21–22). Talking about His resurrection. THAT was to be "the sign". That would be His credentials.

(2)

On another page of the Gospel, Jesus complained that a faithless and wicked generation was always asking for a sign from heaven, was always looking for proofs. Well, the only proof, the only "sign" they were going to get was one like the Prophet Jonah's return to the world of living men after three days inside the sea monster (Mt. 12:39–40). For now, never mind about the Jonah story; let's keep our eye on the ball. The point for us to notice here is, that Jesus Christ Himself appealed to His future resurrection as THE sign that would confirm His identity.

III

To be fully credible to the world at large, such a sign would have to have at least some witnesses, someone who could confirm that it had actually happened. Yet, according to the Gospel accounts themselves, no witness was present in the cave-tomb when the body of Jesus came back to life. The tomb was already empty when an angel rolled back the stone (Mt. 28:2). No one even claimed to have been there looking on at the very moment when the resurrection actually happened. All those whom the New Testament calls "witnesses to the resurrection" saw Jesus only later, fully risen. And really: THAT was witnessing enough!

Certain Catholic theologians have confused the People of God by declaring that the resurrection of Christ cannot be called a historical event, "because there were no witnesses." You mean it never happened? "I didn't say that! I just said it cannot be called a historical event." What people hear you saying is that it's not history. And they take that to mean it never really happened. That would be a false statement. Taking our stand on the inspired word of God in the New Testament, we maintain that it is also false to say that "there were no witnesses."

The resurrection did happen! It wasn't a figment of the Apostle's later meditation, their "Easter faith." Peter (among others) insisted that "God raised Jesus—of that, we are witnesses!" (Acts 2:32). In the following chapter, Peter makes the same statement: "God raised Him from the dead—of THAT, we are witnesses!" (Acts 3:15). Earlier on in chapter one, Peter proposes that the Christian community choose a replacement for Judas, someone who would be "together with us, a witness to the resurrection" (Acts 1:22). This was what being an "Apostle" was all about. Yet how could they be witnesses if they were not there when it happened?

Simple, really. People who associated with Jesus before His death, people who subsequently saw Him dead, and then rubbed elbows with Him fully alive afterwards. People who had the experience of talking with Him both before and after Good Friday, talking with Him prior to the Ascension. Such a person could truly testify, "He came back from being dead." These are, in fact, the conditions that Peter laid down (Acts 1:21–22) for a "Judas-replacement witness"—one of the official group of witnesses.

Such testimony would have to be accepted in any court of law that takes witnesses seriously. Can you swear He came back to life after being publicly executed? I saw Him repeatedly, talked to Him, listened to Him, touched Him. He was very much alive during those six weeks after His crucifixion. Maybe it was just a double, a look-alike? You couldn't fool me: I knew Him for years. Since the baptism of John. Jesus was dead, and He came back from the dead. I can swear to that. It was really "Him"!

That, according to the record (Acts 1–2–3), was the apostles' own understanding of their role. Witnesses to the resurrection of Christ. Witnesses, so that we, too, might believe.

Thomas Doubting, Then Believing
Gospel for Second Sunday of Easter, Years A, B, C
(Lect. 43–44–45)

Each year on the Sunday after Easter, we read the same Gospel selection from the 20th chapter of St. John. This is the part that tells how Jesus visited the Apostles in the Upper Room, both on the evening of Easter Sunday when Thomas was not with them and then again "one week later"—as this Sunday after Easter is one week later—at which time, Thomas WAS there. He could not have known that as a result of John's story, he was about to go down in history as "Doubting Thomas."

I

Doubting Thomas, because he proved so hard to convince that the Lord Jesus had really risen from the dead. Thomas had not been around for the Easter Sunday visit, so when he showed up again, the other Apostles excitedly told him, "Thomas, you missed it! We have seen the Lord!"

Here, as also in John 11:16 and 14:5, Thomas comes through as a realist, a practical person with both feet all-too-firmly planted on the ground. So the Master has returned bodily to life, come alive again after dying on Golgatha? Come on! Oh, so you touched His risen body, did you? Felt it, to make sure it was flesh and bone and not some ghost (Lk. 24:39)? You say that He even showed you in His hands the nail holes left by the crucifixion, and that He still had a wound in His side from the soldier's spear (Jn. 20:20)? Well, just let me see those wounds myself, let me touch them personally. Then I too will believe! Otherwise . . .

II

It was a challenge, a dare, that the Risen Lord accepted. Once again it is the first day of the week. Once again the Apostles have gathered in the Upper Room where they took their leave of Christ the day before He died. Another Sunday evening, one week later. Only this time, Thomas was there. There with his companions.

A lesson here for modern Christian people? If you want to meet the Lord, you had better be with the Christian community on Sundays. Join your fellow disciples on the first day of the week. Thomas missed the first Sunday, and Thomas missed seeing the Lord. Thomas was there with the others on the second Sunday, and Jesus met him there.

When Jesus does drop by the Upper Room, that second Sunday, He focuses His attention on Thomas the Doubter. The Doubter whom He is about to transform into Thomas the Believer.

We could be wrong, but the Lord does not seem to be displeased with His skeptical friend. Amused maybe, but not angry. In fact, Jesus seems to be teasing Thomas. As always, the Master knows how to deal with each of His followers in a personalized way, a way that takes each one's individual make-up into consideration. He will treat Peter like Peter, John like John. And Thomas? This one needed hard evidence; Thomas wanted proof that he could understand. So the Lord gives it to him. We seem to sense Jesus letting Thomas be Thomas, Jesus accepting this disciple where He finds him.

So, Thomas! You wanted to feel My wounds? Go ahead! Put your finger where your mouth was. . . . Thomas knows when he is beaten. Always the realist, he sees that his bluff has been called. So Thomas capitulates. "My Lord and my God!" he says.

Says a lot in a few words. This is an act of faith, this is an act of adoration ("my God"), this is an act of submission ("my Lord"). It's a magnificent prayer! Too bad subsequent generations did not freeze-frame Thomas like this, instead of letting him go down in history (and in *Webster's Dictionary!*) as "Doubting Thomas"!

"Doubting"? Sure, he did that, at first. But then he believed. Even his initial disbelief was a good thing. Saint Gregory the Great commented (quoted in the Liturgy of Hours, Office of Readings for July 3) that the doubt of Thomas did more to confirm our faith than the instant belief of the other Apostles. In other words, it was good to have somebody present who was notoriously hard to convince. Because when such a witness WAS convinced, despite his natural skepticism, it removed all possible doubt forever.

So we join Thomas the Believer in his act of faith and adoration. We join him in his priceless prayer, which says so much that we want to say, and says it in so few words. "My Lord and my God!" Faith and adoration, awe and wonder. Absolute and unconditional surrender. I believe, Lord! Even without seeing the wounds of Your crucifixion; even without the firm feel of Your really resurrected body. You are truly "my Lord and my God"! And I love it.

By the way, Lord: Please thank Thomas for the wonderful prayer he coined for us, the one we borrowed from him and have used so many times. Tell him we are going to use it a dozen more times this very day, and many many times after! Thomas the Realist got it right. You truly are MY LORD AND MY GOD!

Peter Goes Fishing
Gospel for Third Sunday of Easter, Year C
(Lect. No. 48)

Week by week, the Liturgy of the Word sets certain pages of the Bible before us, to be read out officially at the Mass. Through these scripture passages, Christ Himself is speaking to us (Vat. II, Liturgy n. 7). Christ is addressing the whole congregation and every individual in it. What message might He have for us in this post-Easter scene in which Peter goes fishing? Goes fishing, and comes up empty, only to receive a super-catch from the Lord.

I

Seven of the disciples are hanging out together when Peter gets the urge to go fishing. The others decide to go along, not just for the ride but to help him fish. Now, just suppose one or two or three of the seven had decided not to go along. After all, it was going to be work—Peter was a commercial fisherman, not just a sportsman. And it was going to be an all-night job. Surely it would be quite understandable if someone had said, "Well, good luck! See you later!" And then gone home.

It certainly would not have been a sin. Not even blameworthy. And yet, by passing up Peter's venture, they would have missed out on an encounter with the Risen Lord. Not to mention missing one of the most momentous fishing trips in all of history. Something to tell their grandchildren about (if they had any).

100

Moral? Go along with your friends on THEIR project. Help your spouse, your son or daughter and friends with THEIR idea. Even if it would not be your first choice of something to do. Go fish!

II

The seven of them labor all night. No luck. No fish! Nothing. And yet, the biggest haul of their career is waiting for them as soon as the night is past. Life can be like that for you and me. Maybe all our work, all our best efforts, will yield no results. Reading this Gospel can make us realize that the Lord is perfectly capable of producing those results, more abundant and more excellent than we ever dreamed. After we've decided it's hopeless.

Will He do it? It's in His hands. He's under no obligation to make our work successful. However, He might do it anyway, once we have given it our best shot and have nothing to show for it. Could be His way of sending us that same message we find in Jn. 15:5—"Without Me you can do nothing." Pause. "But just watch what happens when I step in!"

III

So far so good. I am not asking for a show of hands, but I have a hunch that just about everybody in church would agree with this general statement, agree with this general principle drawn from the Gospel of St. John. When we are ready to admit that our best efforts won't cut it, there's a chance that the Lord will take over.

Let me go out on a limb, here. (Nobody has to go along.) Because what follows is by no means an official teaching of the Church. It is not contrary to Church teaching either. It's just specu-lation, and as such a lot of people holier and wiser than I am would probably just shake their heads and maybe even smile. Nevertheless . . .

You heard what the Good Lord Jesus had planned for these seven disciples who worked so hard and long and who came up empty. Well, just suppose He had something like that planned for you or me at night's end, at the end of our lives, when day is dawning on the lakeshore of eternity. Our boat is empty, or just about. For seventy or eighty years we have labored away trying to be holy, as the sons and daughters of God ought to be. And we have nothing, or next to nothing, that we can show for it. Like the disciples, we have worked hard all through the night, dutifully trying out all the approved methods taught in the official fisherman's manual, what they teach everywhere in "Holiness 101." It didn't work for us.

At least our lifetime of discipleship has taught us one lesson, one very valuable lesson. Namely, we will never (but never!) be able to pull it off. No effort of ours, no method of anyone, none of it is going to make us holy. We see not only that it DIDN'T, we now understand that it CAN'T. For holiness is grace, and grace is a gift, and gifts are always gratis and often undeserved. Especially if the Giver of the Gift is God, God Who owes us nothing.

So, what if He decided to withhold His gift all through our life-time, to keep us from imagining that our own skill and efforts have built such a splendid house, or filled a net with such fine fish? With the help of God, naturally! He helped, but we did it. . . .

So, what if He was deciding to wait and give it all at once, at the very end? Fill our little ship just as we are approaching shore, fill it to the point where it could not possibly hold another fish? He certainly COULD do that! Will He? I can't swear to it, but I'm telling you I wouldn't put it past Him.

Obviously, this is NOT to suggest that we sit sailing tranquilly (and idly) along, doing nothing while waiting for Him to step in. For it is a safe assumption that if we do nothing, He won't either. Our hope, our fantasy, that He will take over applies only if we are able to borrow the words that Peter used on another similar occasion (Lk. 5:5): "Master, we have labored all night long, and have caught nothing." Only when there is nothing to show for our efforts despite the fact that we DID make efforts. . . . Only THEN does the Good Lord say, "Let down the net once more." And He might not say that until we, like Peter, are within wading distance of the shore. He doesn't need a lot of time to accomplish in a minute what He could have done gradually over the course of our lifetime.

IV

A parting shot: It is interesting that John the Contemplative is the one who recognizes Jesus "on the shore dimly seen through the mists of the deep." But it is Peter, the Man of Action, who jumps overboard and wades ashore, eager to embrace the Risen Lord before He goes and disappears again.

Without contemplatives to discern the Lord and to point Him out, there would be no worthwhile action in the Church on earth. No one leaping out of the still-sailing boat, leaping forward to embrace Christ. However, without people like Peter, there would be ONLY contemplation, and that sounds more like the Church in Heaven than like a Church still plowing the rough seas of this world.

Both types of people are needed in the Church here below. Those with the insight to see, and those who act on what has been seen. Nor should we fail to note that John and the others, the six less impulsive than Peter, they all reached the same shore themselves just a few minutes later. And they had the fish! They, too, shared breakfast with the Risen Lord on the beach. They shared as well in the miraculous catch of fish He provided, provided for them because they, too, had worked all night.

The Ascension
Acts Reading Years A, B, C (Lect. No. 58)

The First Reading for the Feast of the Ascension is from Acts Chapter One. It is the same in all three liturgical cycles, A-B-C. Both here and in Luke's Gospel account of the Ascension, the Lord Jesus is quoted as calling the Apostles "witnesses." In Acts 1:8, He says to them: "You will be My *witnesses.*" Similarly, in the Gospel of Luke (24:48): "You are *witnesses* of these things."

I

This term, "witnesses," sheds a special light on the Ascension of the Lord in the sight of His astonished Apostles. Not only on WHAT happened that day, but on WHY it happened the way it did. If they were to testify before the world that Christ had returned to His Heavenly Father, that fact had to be brought to their own attention in such a way that they would understand it. Understand it with no possibility of a mistake. Our contention is the *way* it happened did just that.

They were *witnesses* of the event, first of all. According to divinely inspired Scripture, THAT was the Apostles' role (Acts 1:21-22), *that* was to be the principal role or "job" of being an Apostle. First and foremost, they where chosen to be official witnesses. To be people who could testify from their own experience, was they themselves observed, from their own personal contact with the Lord Jesus, testify about what He was like, what He taught and what He did. Witnesses not only to His teaching but (principally) to His death and resurrection. Witnesses, finally, to His Ascension into heaven: his ultimate return to the God from Whom He had come.

Therefore, it was in the presence of these Apostles, these witnesses, that the Ascension took place. It was, so to speak, played out for their benefit—not for ours. The Apostles that day were given a message, an experience that they could testify to. If we who come after have any questions, we have to ask the Apostles. What sort of message did the Ascension convey to *them?*

II

The real message was this: Christ Who had come from God, went back to God (Jn. 13:3). Returned to His Heavenly Father once His visible mission on earth had ended. What actually conveyed this message to the Apostles on that day? It was not really direction "up." What was so special about that? What message did they get from seeing a *cloud* receive and envelope their Lord?

We have to realize that this message was being directed at men familiar with the Old Testament. An Old Testament in which a cloud was a repeated and familiar sign of God on special occasions. Nobody thought that God was in every cloud that formed in their skies. Still less did they imagine that God *was* a cloud—or vice versa. It was only that, on certain special occasions when God chose to make them aware of His presence, He came hidden in a cloud. An anonymous author of a medieval spiritual classic found deep meaning in that.

So a special cloud was, in the Old Testament, a special sign that "God is here." For instance, He was in the protecting cloud that shielded the fleeing Israelites from the Egyptian army that was pursuing them (Ex. 14:19–20). Then, on their march through the desert toward the promised land they were led by a pillar of cloud going before them (Ex. 13:21–22). On reaching Mount Sinai, Moses entered into a cloud for a momentous forty-day summit meeting in which he negotiated the covenant-contract between Yahweh and His people (Ex. 20:21).

Much later, King Solomon built a Temple, a House for the Lord; built it on Mount Zion in Jerusalem. When it was finished, God moved into His House under cover of a shining mist, and all the priests had to yield sway to his Divine Majesty present in the cloud (1 Kgs. 8:10–12).

Still later, on another mountain, Peter, James, and John, would hear the voice of the Eternal Father booming out of a cloud. They were overcome with awe, realizing both then and afterwards (2 Pt. 1:18) that this was God speaking: God telling them from within the cloud that this Jesus was His own Beloved Son (Mt. 17:5; Mk. 9:7; Lk. 9:35).

Consequently, when Jesus was raised up into a *cloud* that took Him from their sight, they knew at once that this was not just any old cloud. It was a sign of God the Father, to Whom He was returning.

Returning to His Heavenly Father! That is what the cloud was all about. He must have spoken about it on previous occasions, spoken mysteriously about some forthcoming "return." Recall His words to Mary Magdala, words spoken in the Garden on the day of His resurrection, when she grabbed Him and held on for dear life so He would not get away again, would not just disappear as suddenly as He had appeared. Hey! Don't hold on so tight! I'm not leaving just yet: "I have not yet gone back, not yet ascended, to My Father" (Jn. 20:17). That ascent would be the final act, His definitive departure from the world of men (and women). So on Easter Sunday, He tells Mary Magdalene, that He isn't leaving just yet. You needn't be afraid that I am going to disappear on you right now. There is in the *New American Bible* a footnote to Lk. 24:50–53 to the effect that Luke is putting the Ascension on the night of Easter Sunday. The text does not read way to the unbiased

106

reader, especially one who accepts the same Luke as authoring both Luke's Gospel and the chapter in Acts that plainly describes the Ascension as occurring forty days later. Naturally, the scholars have furnished a footnote there to explain how "forty days" doesn't actually mean forty real days. If anyone wishes to accept these footnotes, they are of course at liberty to do so. But by the same token, the rest of us should be left at liberty to accept what the Scripture actually says, especially since we are given no good reason why we should not.

It wasn't only to Mary Magdalene that the Lord Jesus talked about leaving the world to go back to His Father. In Jn. 16:28, He says to His Apostles "From the Father, I came into the world; I will be leaving the world again, going back to My Father." When it did happen, and a *cloud* took their Lord into itself, they must have remembered and realized that this was it. This was His definitive departure. This was the "return to God" that He had spoken of.

If our interpretation is correct, the direction "up" is not what mattered to the Apostles on Ascension Hill, though that is the element our modern minds have fastened on. For them, going up (up to what our Bible Scholars insist on calling "the sky" so they won't have to mention "heaven") . . . THAT was just incidental. What carried the message about the Lord's return to God the Father (wouldn't "heaven" describe that better than "the sky"?) the real message came from His being received into a *cloud*. That happened to be "up," over their heads: in more ways (and heads) than one.

By latching onto the "up" direction, our modern imaginations have created a pseudo problem about where is heaven "UP?" In "the sky"? Where is "up" in a universe without any "up" or "down"? Where, for that matter, is "the sky" in our universe as we know it? A universe where people in Australia and people in England who were all pointing "up" would in fact be pointing in opposite directions. So how do you point to heaven? Their pointing fingers would signal different and opposite astral regions as they pointed, constantly changing as the earth whirls on its orbit around the sun. . . . No, you can't really locate heaven as "up there." Nor does the Lord's ascension prove that it is in an "up" direction at all.

Like us, the Apostles were also living in such a "pointless" universe, even if they were not as aware of it as we can be. What they *were* aware of was what King Solomon is reported to have said (1 Kgs. 8:12 and 2 Chr. 6:1): "The Lord God dwells in a cloud." Even for Solomon, the cloud was not "up" in a "sky." This was a cloud that had filled his temple with the glory of God.

Which the Apostles must have understood, being Bible people. Whence their testimony, a testimony that they as official witnesses were able to pass on to us. Passed it on, so that we might believe—though there will always be those who won't believe it. What is that testimony? "After completing His mission on earth, Christ the Lord returned to His Father in heaven." We hope to follow Him there.

Pentecost
Years A, B, C (Lect. No. 63)

When we Christians think of Pentecost, we are accustomed to think about the Holy Spirit. More specifically: we recall how the Holy Spirit, the Paraclete, came upon the Church in tongues of fire at her beginning. An older generation of Catholics was even taught to think of Pentecost as being the real "birthday" of the Church.

None of this is wrong. Every year, even in our current three-year cycle of scripture readings, Reading I in the Liturgy of the Word is always this same reading that you have just heard, a reading taken from the second chapter of the Acts of the Apostles. This is what the Bible itself tells us about the coming of the Holy Spirit. What it tells us about the First Christian Pentecost.

However, the first *Christian* Pentecost was not the first Feast of Pentecost, period! Jewish People and the Jewish religion had already been celebrating a Pentecost Feast for many generations before ours. Devout Jews still celebrate it today under the Hebrew name Shavuot, which means "Feast of Weeks." Perhaps by looking at what it means for them, we can gain a better understanding of what it ought to mean for us.

Shavuot, the Feast of Weeks. Weeks, like the seven-day period of time that we are familiar with. Going back to the Old Testament Book of Exodus, we read there the story of how God liberated His Chosen People from servitude in Egypt. That liberation gave them their first and greatest feast, Passover (Pesach, Pasch).

Seven weeks later, seven times seven days later, they came to

Mount Sinai (aka Horeb), where Jahweh made a Covenant-contract with them through their leader and spokesman, Moses. That Covenant, that contract between God and His People, is
basically what *we* call "the Old Testament." In three separate sacred books (Exodus, Leviticus, and Deuteronomy), the Jewish
people are ordered to commemorate this, their contract with the
Lord, by celebrating an annual Feast of Weeks.

That Feast of Weeks became their Number Two religious
holiday and holy day. It was a feast that ranked right after Passover
in importance, a feast that followed Passover by an interval of
seven weeks, seven-times-seven days, just like their trek from the
Red Sea to Mt. Horeb.

In the same way, our present Christian Feast of Pentecost follows Easter for us, and depends upon *its* timing. Our "Easter Season" stretches between the one feast and the other as an interval of
seven weeks (seven-times-seven-plus-a-day, and the next day
then becomes the "50th"—which is what the Greek word "Pentecost" actually means).

II

There seems to be a message here, a message for us in God's
choosing this anniversary of the Old Covenant to give us a New
One. A New Covenant (Heb. 8:13), with Jesus instead of Moses as
mediator (Heb 8:6), and all the world as "the party of the second
part" in the contract, instead of merely the Twelve Tribes of Israel.
"Go make disciples of *all* the nations," said the Lord; that was His
parting word to His Church (Mt. 28:19).

We live in a day when a striving for political correctness
looms larger than respect for what has been taught always and everywhere by everyone (*semper et ubique et ab omnibus*). Wherefore some theologians of the past twenty years will vehemently
resist our saying (with Christians of the past twenty centuries) that

the New Testament has *replaced* the Old. We may be accused of ignorance, even of "anti-Semitism." Haven't we read the recent writings of European theologians and exegetes (like Lohfink), the decrees of Vatican II (like Non-Christians), or even the new Catholic Catechism that states (n. 121) that "the Old Covenant has never been revoked?" On the other hand, when comparing covenants, old and new, or when contrasting Jesus to Moses as mediator, the Epistle to the Hebrews is pretty clear. For instance, it reads: "In speaking of a 'new' covenant, He declares the first one *obsolete*" (Heb. 8:13). And: "He (Jesus) is Mediator of a *better covenant,* enacted on better promises" (Heb. 8:6).

This is not the place to go into all the distinctions and the fine details that would be necessary to solve such a complicated theological problem. We only want to warn you that it exists, and that not everyone will be happy with our assertion that a New-Testament Covenant *has taken the place of the Old. Not all moderns, Jewish or Christian, will appreciate the fact* that the reign of Moses as Mediator of the Covenant has now ended. That Christ the God-Man is firmly in place as the sole and definitive Mediator between mankind and God his Heavenly Father (1 Tim. 2:5). Not everyone is going to like the new arrangement whereby there is a New People of God instead of a special Chosen People limited by race and ethnicity. Even in apostolic times, it was hard for some people to get the message that there was now a *new testament* (*new covenant*) in place of the old one with its rituals and regulations. St. Paul's raging fights against "Judaizers" and "the Law" bear witness to the struggle (see Galatians & Acts, not only Romans!).

In at least two documents (Church n. 16 and Non-Christians n. 4) the Second Vatican Council declares that the Jews "remain most dear to God" because of their fathers. Nonetheless, it seems to us that God's own timing of the Christian Pentecost does convey a clear message about a new covenant.

The New People of God, under the New Covenant, now embraces potentially the whole human family. That message was conveyed in another way also on Pentecost Day: the polyglot assortment of pilgrims present for the First Christian Pentecost. They came from present-day Iraq and Iran and Turkey, as well as North Africa.

Most of the places mentioned in Acts 2:9–11 are overwhelmingly Muslim today. Descendants of those First Pentecost pilgrims have rejected Christ in favor of Mohammed. That is really sad. Perhaps we should pray that the Holy Spirit may descend upon them in our own time, to make them convinced followers of the Lord Christ.

It looks impossible. But we who once lived in the era of world communism thought it impossible to overthrow *that* too. Where is the Iron Curtain now? The Wall of Berlin? The Comintern? Really, for God, nothing is out of question (Lk. 1:37). Nothing at all.

Corpus Christi
Exodus Reading Year B Lect. No. 168
Gospel B (168) & Corinthians C (169)

I

On a Thursday forty days after Easter, the Church remembers how Christ her Lord ascended into heaven, returning to His Father. On another Thursday three weeks later, the Thursday after Trinity Sunday, the Church keeps a solemn feast of His eucharistic body and blood. A feast designed to remind us that Christ remains with us here on earth even after officially leaving us for heaven.

Two Thursdays. However, in places like ours where any Thursday will normally be a school day and a work day, the celebration of both feasts is moved to the Sunday following. That way all Catholics can be in church and can get both messages. Christ has gone ahead: Ascension. Christ remains with us in the Eucharist: the Feast of His Body-and-Blood, which used to be called "Corpus Christi." Body of Christ. Even by people who didn't know Latin.

II

Nowadays, it is the Feast of His Body AND HIS BLOOD. After seven centuries of officially calling it Corpus Christi ("Body of Christ"), the name of the feast has now been officially changed to include His blood. Because all the People of God now have the option of receiving Holy Communion under *both* forms, to drink from the chalice as well as to receive the sacred host. This (we are told) was the ancient custom, one that has been revived in our own time after centuries of disuse.

Those were centuries during which some rebels protested that the laity were not receiving the *whole* Christ, and the Church stoutly maintained that they were. Our story is that this position of the Church was confirmed by a miracle, and that miracle gave rise to the Feast of Corpus Christi, a full seven hundred years before the Second Vatican Council. It is a story that is both humanly and historically reliable, and one that makes excellent good sense in the context of history—even if it may bother some people who are loath to take miracles seriously.

III

Around the year 1400, certain university professors in Bohemia were teaching that Christ was not entirely present in just one eucharistic form alone, but only in both taken together. Therefore they said, to really receive the Lord sacramentally it was necessary to give the "chalice to the laity." That became a war cry. "The chalice to the laity." Pitched battles were actually fought in the present-day Czech Republic, though of course political motives got mixed with the religious ones. Finally, the Council of Constance came out with a formal solemn definition of faith, affirming that taking communion under only one form was indeed receiving the whole Christ (Session xiii, 15 June 1415).

By then, the controversy had been going on a long time, and it bothered the faith of a lot of people. One such tortured soul was a priest of Bohemia. Torn by doubt, this priest decided to make the long pilgrimage over the Alps on foot, to the Tomb of the Apostle Peter in Rome, where he would pray for peace. For peace, and for faith in the practice of the Church. He got his answer a bit early. At Lake Bolsena, some 60 miles north of Rome, but very close to where the pope was staying at the time.

There on the shore of Lake Bolsena, our priest stopped to offer Mass at the tomb of an early Christian girl-martyr. There the Consecrated Host dripped blood on the altar linen for him—Christ was letting him know that the Host alone also held His blood. The incident would later be immortalized in the Vatican's Stanze di Raffaello, where even today tourists can admire a fresco called La Messa di Bolsena, without having a clue what it is all about. (The pope shown on the fresco is not Urban IV who was pope then, in the mid-1200s, but rather, it is Julius II—Raphael's boss!)

To answer the sophisticated, who will smile at our naivete: Yes, we are aware that stories about bleeding hosts abounded in medieval times. Usually, though, they had another genesis: often to accuse Jews of sacrilegiously profaning the Sacred Host. And all those other stories do not fit into a historical context like the Miracle of Bolsena, which happened for a priest from that region, a region where the question was not just the Real Presence of Christ in the sacrament, but the presence of His blood in the sacred host.

At the time of the miracle in 1263, Pope Urban IV and his court were not in Rome, but in the secure fortress city of Orvieto, not far from Bolsena. The Pope called for the blood-stained altar linen. He must have been convinced about what happened, because on August 11, 1264, he issued a decree instituting the Feast of Corpus Christi. St. Thomas Aquinas, one of the greatest theologians ever, was teaching theology at the papal court at that time. Pope Urban commissioned him to compose a liturgical office for the new feast. Part of it was a sequence that is still in our liturgy today.

The citizens of Orvieto must have been convinced as well, or they would never have built such a magnificent cathedral to house the relic. (The writer saw the relic in the early 1950s.) It should be noted that there wasn't time for a legend to grow up; it was only about a year from the fact to the feast. Nor do we have the usual earmarks that characterize legends: vagueness about the time and place, for instance. There's nothing vague here.

IV

Some moderns are allergic to miracles, and that is their privilege. For them, we would like to add a link between today's feast and the Bible. Words from the Bible (Lk. 22:20 and 1 Cor. 11:25), words of Christ that you hear at every Mass: "A new covenant IN MY BLOOD." What's the connection between a covenant and blood?

In the Book of Exodus (24:5–8) we read how the Old Covenant, the contract between God and His People, was sealed in blood, victim blood that was sprinkled on the people and on the altar. The altar stood for God. The Covenant was a blood pact between the people and Him. Well, the NEW Covenant, the NEW Testament, which is OUR contract with God, has also been sealed with blood. The blood of the victim Christ. The blood that we commemorate today, on the Feast of His Body and Blood. Victim body, victim blood. Our covenant is sealed in the blood of Christ.

The Christ of God
Gospel for XII Sunday Ordinary Time, Year C
(Lect. No. 96)

When we meditate upon our weekly Gospel readings, there are two sorts of questions that we ought to keep in mind: (1) What does this particular scripture reading have to say to the world at large? (What does it really MEAN?) And, (2) What is it saying to me? (What does it mean for ME?)

I

First of all, what does the text really mean, taken by itself? What is its meaning as it stands in the Bible setting? To find an answer, there are several methods that we might employ.

One way would be to go back to the original wording. Now, with the probable exception of Matthew, our Gospels were originally written in Greek. Biblical Greek. So if we want to know what some obscure passage really says, we have to find out what those Greek words mean: what they meant back then.

Now there are all sorts of books that can help you with that, if you have them handy and if you are able to read Greek. Or at least able to decipher the Greek alphabet, which leaves out most grass-roots Christians in our part of the world, people who not specialized in that sort of study. So they have to take what the missalette says. Or, with a little bit of good fortune and a library handy, they might be adventurous enough to see how other translators put it. How some other people understood the meaning of the problem text.

For instance: in our NAB American version, the Gospel says that Jesus "rebuked" the Apostles. It seems strange that He would do that. Rebuke them, scold them, for having acknowledged Him to be the Messiah. Well, we don't have to believe that He was scolding them at all. A quick check through ten other English translations shows half of them rendering the word as "strict orders." The Douay-Rheims, the King James, and one other use the word "strictly"; none of them call it a rebuke.

Turning to Greek dictionaries, one finds that the original word CAN mean "to rebuke." It can also mean to give someone strict orders. From the context of this Gospel verse, it is evident that the latter is preferable here. Jesus was not displeased with the faith of His disciples; however, He did not want them spreading the word just yet. He did not want to create an army of political backers who might possibly interfere with His future passion and death, something that He mentions here almost in the same breath.

So the context becomes important for us to avoid getting the wrong impression. In addition to a word-study, the context is always an important way to find out the real meaning of a scripture text. The "con-text" is what goes with a text: its surroundings, its setting. Here, for instance, Jesus immediately brings up His future passion and death, thus giving us a hint WHY the Apostles were not to tell anyone yet that He was the Messiah.

A broader context than just one page is the whole context of the Bible. The editor's footnotes will usually show you where else to look. For example, what we read here in Luke Chapter 9 is also to be found in Matthew Chapter 16 and Mark Chapter 8. In all three places, Jesus asks, "What are people saying about Me?" and then: "What do YOU say?"

In all three Gospel versions, Mt.-Mk.-Lk., the buzz is this: that the general public is undecided. What about you, the Inner Circle of Disciples? In all three Gospels, it is Peter-the-Impulsive

118

who gives an answer for them all: Jesus is indeed The Messiah, The Christ. Matthew's version then adds something special: ". . . The Christ, the SON OF THE LIVING GOD."

Some scholars are reluctant to admit that such an acknowledgment of Christ as God was indeed part of Peter's original confession. They opine that any statement of Christ's divinity must have been added a generation or so later, when the Gospel was written. How could Peter have come to believe, so early on, that Jesus was really the very Son of God?

The context in Matthew already answers their problem—unless these scholars want to maintain that the context, too, was fabricated by a later generation of believers. For in that Matthean context (16:17) Jesus directly says that "flesh and blood" (= human means) had not provided Peter with this insight: it came to him as a revelation from God. If anyone does not want to accept this answer from the scripture text itself, that is his or her problem.

II

In these two ways, the meaning of words and their setting in this particular context, we can learn a great deal about what the Bible is actually saying. From here, we can take a further step and ask, what is it saying to us? What are the practical consequences for my life? What do I keep on doing and what changes do I make?

One practical conclusion might be this: We will not just shape our ideas according to what other people are saying. We will not just accept what "everybody knows." Conventional wisdom is often wrong, as it was in the case of Christ. People thought He might be John the Baptist, or Elijah, or one of the ancient prophets, when actually He was none of the above.

Conventional wisdom is communicated by journalists in a modern media world. Such conventional wisdom might contradict what the Church is trying to teach us. Modern views on abortion, divorce, ideal family size, clerical celibacy, women priests, gay marriage . . . You name it, and the media has a view they are trying to sell. Well, today's public opinion can be just as wrong about such matters as public opinion once was wrong about the shape of the earth.

That would be one lesson. Don't necessarily go by what everyone is saying. A second lesson, even more valuable, would be this: go with Peter. Two ways. One way for sure: We renew our faith in Christ, not only as Savior and Messiah and Leader, but also as the very Son of God. That is already clearly in the creed we recite on Sundays after the homily. The other way would be this: listen to Peter's successor, the pope, who lives over there, just a few yards from where Peter's body is buried, in Rome.

The Prodigal Son
Gospel for Fourth Sunday of Lent, Year C
(Lect. No. 33)

The Bible tells us (Mt. 13:34; Mk. 4:33–34) that Jesus taught the people by means of parables. A parable is basically a comparison. Christ the Lord compared the unseen world of the spirit to the familiar world people knew from their everyday lives. He could point to a farmer sowing wheat, a woman making bread, fishermen casting their nets in the lake, children playing in the city streets. Everywhere He looked, He saw reflected "the Kingdom of Heaven."

I

Sometimes His hearers missed the point, and so do we. Take for example the "Parable of the Prodigal Son" in Lk. 15:11–32. Known to generations of Christians as "The Prodigal," this wayward lad has become "The Lost Son" in our NAB version: the idea probably being to parallel the other losses featured in the same chapter (lost sheep, lost coin, lost son). What impressed our frugal ancestors was the young man's prodigality—the word actually means extravagance in spending one's material resources. Which is at most a side issue in Jesus' story: not the main point at all.

What IS the main point? Some people suggested that the parable might be better entitled, the Parable of the Merciful Father. This would be closer, since Christ evidently intended to convey the idea that God is more merciful to sinners than their fellow sinners are. And that there is more joy in heaven over a sinner's return than there is here on earth (see verses 7 and 10).

And yet, the larger context of St. Luke's fifteenth chapter seems to suggest that the Lord Jesus was actually making another point, another comparison. He was comparing the Scribes and Pharisees to the third character in the story, the elder brother, the "good guy," sulking because his spendthrift brother had been welcomed home.

Early in the chapter, before the lost-sheep-lost-coin-lost-brother parables, tax collectors and other sinners are flocking to Jesus, and the good people are grumbling about it. "This man even accepts sinners, He actually eats with them!" Such complaints would explain the addition of verses 25–32 to the Lost Son Parable. Another dimension is thereby given to the lesson already conveyed by the other two parables (the sheep and the coin), which speak of joy in heaven because God gets back a straying sinner. In all three cases, God rejoices. But good people . . . ? Verses 25–32.

II

This focus on the Elder Son, this lesson aimed at the grumblers of verse one, does it mean that the parable *cannot* contain any other message? For untold generations of Christians and for the Liturgy itself, the story Jesus told has always been a classic invitation to conversion. Turn back to God: you will be received kindly. Is that interpretation "out" since the emphasis on the grumblers is "in"?

Not at all. As remarked elsewhere in this book, the words of Scripture can have more than one meaning. And the exhortation to conversion, focusing on the Father and on His returning prodigal son: such an application of the parable has a long history of saints, preachers, and writers undoubtedly filled with the Spirit of God. O "prodigals," sinners, have no fear! This story is for you, too.

For there can in fact be more than one lesson taught by the parable, and no one is obliged to choose "either/or"—either a traditional emphasis on the younger son OR a new emphasis on the elder one. Take a modern example, a modern "parable" if you will. When the Federal Reserve came out with a new type of $50 or $20 bill, you did not have to discard the old fifties and twenties in your wallet simply because there was a new bill you had never seen before. No "either/or" decision was required. You do have to be careful, lest the different-looking bill be counterfeit, worthless. So you take a close look at BOTH kinds, the old and the new; you keep all that are good.

III

That said, let's go one step farther. An additional step, it is true, but one still in line with the theme of the Merciful Father. One still focusing the spotlight on the goodness and kindness of a loving and forgiving God. Something that Jesus definitely taught!

When the wayward son decides to return home and throw himself on his father's mercy, he rehearses a little speech he will make, one he hopes will turn aside parental wrath. "Father," he says, "I have sinned. . . . No longer worthy to be called your son . . . Take me on as one of the hired hands. . . ."

A fine speech, surely, and well thought out. And yet, the way Jesus tells the story, the boy never got a chance to recite the whole carefully crafted act of contrition. When he is only as far as being unworthy to be called a son, his father cuts off the speech and begins issuing orders to the servants for a welcome-home party.

Suppose you're dying. You're about to face God, and you figure you have some explaining to do. So you rack your brains trying to remember the act of contrition—you just hope you'll get it right.

Now wouldn't it be great if, when your soul approaches your Father's House, the Father Himself runs out to meet you. He cuts off your anxious act of contrition with a hug and a kiss. "Yes, yes," He says, "I know. But you're here now, and that's all that matters. So glad you could make it! As for those past wrong turns, that stumbling you did, those falls, those wrong choices . . . it doesn't matter now. Say no more! Welcome home, child! Come right on in. Your place at the table is all set for you, your cup runneth over. I'm so glad!"

Call this a fantasy if you will. But don't surprised if it turns out that way for you and for me. I really hope that it will!

Casting the First Stone

Gospel for Fifth Sunday of Lent, Year C (Lect. No. 36)

I

In St. Luke's Gospel, Chapter 15, there are three parables about God's mercy towards sinners. These three parables, according to Lk. 15:1–2, were prompted by good people complaining that "the bad guys" found Jesus so approachable. So non-judgmental.

At one point, it seems that His enemies decided they could use this attitude of the Lord to get Him into trouble. They would set things up in such fashion that He would lose face no matter which way He reacted. The story is told in John's Gospel, chapter eight.

They were about to stone a woman to death for adultery. They had the Law on their side, and stones already in their hands. But first, they dragged the unlucky lady before Jesus, and piously asked for His opinion. After first reminding Him that "Moses in the Law" (Jn 8:5) had prescribed the death penalty for such a one. What do YOU say? Choose between your mercy and the Law!

All the world knows what Jesus said: "Let someone without sin cast the first stone" (Jn. 8:7). There were no takers. Since the Only One Who Qualified was not casting any stones, the woman was free to go. "I am not going to condemn you," said Jesus. "Just don't do it again" (Jn. 8:11).

II

It would be a mistake to conclude from this incident that adultery was no big deal in Jesus' book. He DOES tell the woman not to commit this sin anymore. But as for "zero tolerance," He seemed rather to believe in giving people a second chance, even sending her back to the same neighborhood.

The main point, though, is this: sins CAN be forgiven. Even such a sin as this one, which married people find so hard to forgive, God forgives, even though His Ten Commandments did rank, "Thou shalt not commit adultery," right up there alongside of "Thou shalt not kill."

And when God walked the earth in human form, He condemned the sin of adultery, but not the sinner herself. Her sin was one of the sixteen crimes for which "Moses in the Law" had decreed the death penalty (Lv. 20:10; Dt. 22:22). In this case, Christ the Lord did not challenge nor change the Mosaic Law, as He did in the case of divorce (Mt. 19:8–9).

III

Sin exists. Sin is real. The laws of God and men are real. Some sins forbidden by the law are still deadly without the law, without any law but the law of nature itself. All sins are wrong, though only some of them are mortally so. "Mortal" means death-dealing. Throughout the ages, capital punishment has been a recognition by most societies that some sins are grave enough to be death-dealing.

Without denying either the reality of sin or the justice of punishment due to sin, the message of Christ is still that there be mercy. Though sin is real, sinners can be forgiven. And fortunately for everyone, God is not as strict as godly people often are. Were the holiness of God to burn more brightly and warmly in His children, they would be less likely to judge, less likely to condemn. Divine Holiness was full in Christ, God's Son: and HE was able to say, "For my part, I will not condemn you" (Jn. 8:11).

IV

Over and above His holiness, His forgiveness, and His mercy, this page of John's Gospel is priceless for something else it tells us about the Master. Two more personal qualities that give us an insight into what Jesus was (and is) like. Let's not leave the scene without taking notice of that!

First of all, how brilliantly He avoided the trap his enemies laid for Him! Was He going to acquiesce in this brutal killing, or would He lose percentage approval points among the people, by despising or at least contradicting the sacred Law of Moses?

Neither. Far from joining them in the throwing of stones, Jesus gave the world a phrase that is worthy of being engraved in stone. They thought they had Him impaled on the horns of a dilemma. Instead, He evaded both horns, and did it so easily, so gracefully, so effortlessly. You've got to admire someone Who could do that, without even getting time to think it over. He's good!

Secondly, note His sense of humor. Serious as the situation was, the would-be judges and executioners must have cut a comical figure as they began to recuse themselves, to drop the rocks they were clutching and slink away one by one. When there is no one left on the scene except for the accused sinner and the Sinless One Who Wouldn't Condemn, Jesus looks up from his doodling in the dust and asks in feigned surprise: "Why! Where did they all go? No one hung around to condemn you?" (Jn. 8:10).

Apparently, the humorous side of the situation was not lost on Christ the Lord. It would be a pity if it were lost on us, because then we would have lost one more insight into the precious human "personality" of Christ the Lord. A likeable Person indeed! May there be more like Him.